MICHAEL HLATKY

BEER Brewing FOR EVERYONE

Schiffer Publishing Ltd®

4880 Lower Valley Road • Atglen, PA 19310

Other Schiffer Books on Related Subjects:

The Perfect Sausage: Making and Preparing Homemade Sausage
Karsten "Ted" Aschenbrandt, hard cover, 120pp. ISBN: 978-0-7643-4302-5. $19.99
The Big Smoker Book
Karsten "Ted" Aschenbrandt and Rudolf Jaeger. ISBN: 978-0-7643-4328-5,
hard cover, 152pp. $34.99
Distilling Fruit Brandy
Josef Pischl. ISBN: 978-0-7643-3926-4, hard cover, 176pp. $34.99

Photo credits: All images were provided by the author.

Originally published as *Bierbrauen für jedermann*
by Leopold Stocker Verlag, Graz - Stuttgart, 2011.
Translated by Omicron Language Solutions, LLC

Type set in ITC Symbol

ISBN: 978-0-7643-4499-2
Printed in China

Published by Schiffer Publishing, Ltd.
4880 Lower Valley Road
Atglen, PA 19310
Phone: (610) 593-1777; Fax: (610) 593-2002
E-mail: Info@schifferbooks.com

For our complete selection of fine books on this and related subjects,
please visit our website at www.schifferbooks.com.
You may also write for a free catalog.

This book may be purchased from the publisher. Please try your bookstore first.

We are always looking for people to write books on new and related subjects.
If you have an idea for a book, please contact us at proposals@schifferbooks.
com.

Schiffer Publishing's titles are available at special discounts for bulk purchases for
sales promotions or premiums. Special editions, including personalized covers,
corporate imprints, and excerpts can be created in large quantities for special needs.
For more information, contact the publisher.

Contents

Foreword

Unbelievably, fifteen years have passed since the first edition of *Beer Brewing for Everyone* was published in Germany. Changes and additions were incorporated into the six editions that followed, but now the time has come for a completely new and revised edition of this—one can calmly state—standard work of home brewing literature. Experience from more than 80 home brewing seminars has been incorporated into the book, as have countless suggestions from enthusiastic readers and home brewers, whose ideas have helped advance the hobby.

Through much devotion, love and knowledge, the hobby has resulted in the creation of small micro breweries with attached taverns or public houses.

In response to numerous requests, the new edition of the book has been expanded to also include recipes that do not comply with the strict rules of the German Purity Law.

> Europe has a vast variety of local and regional specialty beers to offer; one only has to think of Belgian wheat and lambic beers; ales, stouts and porters in England, Guinness in Ireland, Altbiere and Weißbiere in Germany, and even beers made from grains such as rye, spelt or oats.

Until the 19th century a large pot, usually made of copper, was part of every bride's dowry. In addition to making beer, it was also used by housewives for preserving fruit and vegetables and as a wash tub. The rise of commercial brewing with its beer packaged in kegs and bottles resulted in the disappearance of the small, local breweries, but it also caused knowledge about the art of beer brewing passed down through generations to be lost.

In Germany, the Beer Tax Law passed after the Second World War expressly forbade brewing at home and appeared to have delivered a death blow to this ancient tradition. Not until the end of the 1980s, with the reversion to natural practices following the rise of the Green Party and countless food scandals, was there a renaissance of "home made."

The same trend was seen internationally. Suddenly the making of bread, cheese, and jam, the distilling of brandy, the making of wine and home-brewed beer were "in" again. After the Second World War a very active home-brewing scene developed in America and England, as well as in Holland and Belgium, with the establishment of beer-making clubs that resulted in exchanges of recipes and information.

Whereas there was a vast amount of literature containing sometimes obscure beer recipes available in the English language, in German there was almost nothing for hobby brewers. In the mid-1990s I released my two books *Beer Brewing for Everyone* and *Beer Brewing at Home*, which filled this gap for beginners new to the hobby. Meanwhile many home brewers had already organized themselves into clubs and groups of regulars at pubs. Recipes were exchanged over the internet, beer seminars were attended, and makers of small equipment had cautiously accepted the hobby by offering products for home brewers. Mail order businesses also sprang up, offering malt, hops, and yeast in small quantities. In the early days of home brewing in Germany it was almost impossible to obtain raw materials under their proper names. Malt and hops—if available at all—were usually sold as "light malt" or "dark malt" in whole form, the hops with no reference to their bittering substances, and yeast in 7-gram packets identified only as "top-fermenting" or "bottom-fermenting." Obtaining materials from breweries was almost impossible for "competitive reasons" and as yet there were no micro breweries. Nowadays a wide variety of brew shops offer all of the necessary raw materials with appropriate instructions and labels, which has of course increased the complexity of making the decision of what to buy.

There is no limit to the inventiveness and technical skill of the home brewer. Most hobby brewers began with the famous "cooking pot" and "cloth diapers." Many in rural areas used equipment already at hand, such as brandy stills and steamers for brew pots and fermenting equipment used in making wine. Surplus steel kegs from breweries were cut up and converted into fermentation vessels, wells were dug for optimal brewing water, lauter tuns were fashioned from plastic or stainless steel, and elaborate wort chillers were made from copper tubing with hot water recovery systems. In most cases, the cellar or workshop was quickly converted into a miniature brewery for the new hobby. Of all the "brewing machines" I have encountered during my research, one of the most unusual is a converted washing machine. Equipped with an electric drive, an integrated thermostat, and a pump, the washing machine became a fully functional micro brewery in a tiny space.

I have tried out many flavoring ingredients that at first glance seemed surprising—from Christmas beer with cinnamon to oat beer to pumpkin beer. For technical and space reasons, most home brewed beers are top-fermented, however, many home brewers have committed all their enthusiasm to also make bottom-fermented beers, which usually requires an electrical cooling system. Much love and creativity is also expended in making beer caps and labels. The quality of homemade beer differs widely, but in most cases it can stand up well in a comparison with beer from micro breweries and large commercial breweries. As I have discovered during taste-testings at my many beer seminars and visits to private breweries, no expense or effort is spared in the quest for a perfect beer. Some home brewers have developed so-called "mobile breweries," which can be transported from place to place in small trailers or the trunks of cars.

There are also some home brewers who use their home brewing as a step on the way to their own micro brewery. Nowadays a number of agricultural colleges give courses in beer brewing, enjoying the same status as the distilling of brandy or the fermentation of grape juice.

The legal status of beer makers is still unclear. In Austria, some guest houses are operated as taverns, a business that requires the approval of the local community and in particular the mayor. If a farmer grows malting barley, why should he not be able to sell his product? How is beer different than wine, must and brandy? The tax situation as well has yet to be resolved satisfactorily.

In Germany it is still necessary to submit—before brewing—a verbal report to the responsible customs office, while in Austria and Switzerland home brewing is permitted exclusively for private consumption—although no report is necessary.

Happily, it is not just men who are indulging in this new-old hobby. At least one third of the attendees at beer-making events are women, and the number is growing rapidly.

For information about beer brewing seminars and beer events, please consult my website www.verlagsagentur-hlatky.com.

With the old brewer's greeting

"Hopfen und Malz, Gott erhalt's"
(God preserve malt and hops)

I wish you much enjoyment from reading this book
and success in your brewing efforts.

What Is Beer?

Beer is probably the most consumed alcoholic drink and one of the oldest comestibles and stimulants known to mankind. The German Purity Law defines its allowable ingredients—water, malt and hops—in the sixteenth century no one knew that yeast caused fermentation. The German Beer Law and the *Codex Alimentarius Austriacus* provided a somewhat more precise definition of the raw materials. "Beer is a drink produced from cereals, hops, and water by mashing and boiling, fermented by yeast, containing alcohol and carbon dioxide." Cereals were defined as barley, wheat, rice, corn or products of these.

Written in dry legal German, this declaration lists the allowable ingredients and brewing processes for the making of beer. But does this definition really explain what beer is, what significance this beverage had in the past and still has?

Beer is inextricably linked with cultural history, for it was not until humans settled down and began practicing agriculture that they were able to cultivate grains such as emmer, spelt, barley, wheat, rye and oats.

Surplus grain, which was not essential for the production of bread, could be fermented and turned into beer or, more accurately, a beer-like drink. Making beer was then a form of preservation, for "liquid bread" in clay jugs was easier to protect against vermin, mice, and rats than bulk-stored grain, which was defenseless against these parasites.

The following is one of the most plausible explanations as to how man discovered that an alcoholic drink could be made from grain:

Scraps of bread were placed in a container with water, the sun heated the water, and the "wild" yeast spores in the air began the fermentation process. Very soon man began initiating this spontaneous, unplanned process purposefully and intentionally. Even though the bio-chemical process has not changed since then, this beer-like drink resulting from wild fermentation bore no comparison to the refreshing drink we imagine today. Rather these first beers were cloudy and contained remnants of the grains used in the brewing process. The picture "beer-drinking Sumerians" (ca. 3,000 years B.C.) shows them drinking beer through straws to avoid slurping the grain remnants and impurities. The sparkling, refreshing carbon dioxide had also mostly escaped from the beer, to say nothing of the absence of refrigeration in hot regions.

A Brief History of Beer

Archaeological digs in Mesopotamia prove that the Sumerians, Assyrians, and Babylonians were the first beer brewers known to history. The digs in Catal Hüyük in Asia Minor show that the inhabitants of this settlement, one of the oldest known Stone Age habitations, were already familiar with barley beer by around 6,000 B.C. Towards the end of the 4th century BC the Sumerians were using malted grain to bake "grain bread;" this flat bread was then dissolved in water and allowed to ferment. The development of bread making is inseparable from that of beer brewing. Only by activating the enzymes in grain was it possible to turn the starch in the grain into fermentable sugar. This was most easily achieved if the grain was germinated and then baked. The process of converting starch into sugar and then into alcohol was humanity's first biochemical achievement. From a biochemical point of view, the creation of must and wine is much simpler, as the sugar needed for fermentation is already present in the fruit.

King Hammurabi of Babylonia (1728–1686 BC) felt obliged to issue strict brewing and serving regulations to protect his subjects. Today one can admire these statutory provisions, written in cuneiform, in the Louvre in Paris, and paragraphs 108-121 represent the oldest known bar rules in the world. Hammurabi ostensibly created these rules to protect the health of his subjects and prevent price gouging. The serving of watered-down beer was prohibited as was the use of inferior ingredients. An entirely desirable and pleasant side-effect for the rulers was the statutory implementation by these rules of one of the first beer taxes.

A brief excerpt from the martialist text of the statute reads:

- The landlady who accepts payment for beer in silver instead of barley or who sells inferior beer for a high price, will be drowned.
- A priestess who visits a public house, or even opens a public house, will be burned.
- Those who water down their beer will be drowned in their barrels or will have their beer poured down their throats until they drown.

While the penalties have become less severe, the problems of adulteration of beer through the use of poor quality or harmful ingredients and price gouging still remain.

As one can see from this text from King Hammurabi's law, the production of beer was then the domain of women and it would remain so until the Middle Ages, when monks in monastery breweries slowly began forcing women out. In the private sphere—the brewing of beer for domestic consumption—this tradition continued until the early twentieth century. The dowry of every bride included a large pot, usually copper, which could be used for washing clothes but also for the brewing of beer.

In Mesopotamia, not only was beer the main drink, but it was used as a means of barter and payment, and also as a unit of measurement for the payment of workers. Several kinds of beer of different strength and quality were already being brewed.

In Egypt, on the other hand, beer brewing was a state monopoly. Everyone, from the pharaoh downwards through the officers and officials to the slaves, received a precisely-determined quantity of bread and beer according to his social station. Beer in clay jugs was placed in the tombs of the dead, along with food, in order to sustain them during the long journey to the realm of the dead. The Egyptians are known to have made more than twenty kinds of beer, which differed in composition and alcoholic content. Chemical analysis of the remains of these burial goods has revealed the ingredients, and in Egypt

Depiction of a drinking session in the court of King Sargon II of Assyria (721 – 705 BC) in the palace of Dur Sharrukin (Chorsabad).

today these "pharaoh beers" are brewed as a special attraction, although it is doubtful whether they taste anything like the originals. The Greeks, Jews, and, later, the Romans learned the art of brewing beer from the Egyptians.

Whereas the Egyptians regarded beer as a basic foodstuff, among the Greeks and Romans it was—because of climate—supplanted by wine. Roman propaganda discredited beer as a "barbaric drink," mainly because the Celts and Germans, Rome's main foes in Central Europe, were beer drinkers. The Romans preferred wine as the drink of an apparently "higher" civilization. Emperor Julian (331–363 AD) went even further, claiming in a satirical poem that: "Wine smells like nectar, but beer stinks of ram." His successor, Emperor Flavius Valens, on the other hand, enjoyed drinking beer very much. The ancients were, however, very well aware of the medicinal effects of beer. The Greek doctor Hippocrates (approx. 460–377 BC), one of the founders of the medicinal arts, mentioned various medical uses and healing effects of beer.

> Hippocrates recommended beer as a "soothing medium, smooth and steadying, pleasant to take." It quenched the thirst, promoted digestion and elimination, and was also an effective means of combating insomnia, reducing fever, and relieving dehydration.

Celts and Germans did not use hops, which they knew as a vegetable similar to asparagus, to bitter their beer; instead they used much more bitter oak bark, various seasoning herbs, and especially hemp.

Christian monks played a significant role in the development of brewing in Central Europe in the Middle Ages. During the Christianization of Central Europe, Irish monks brought with them the knowledge of how beer is brewed, founding the first monastery breweries in Ettal and St. Gallen in Switzerland. The brewery plans—there were several breweries for various beers in each monastery—of St. Gallen have survived and testify to the already very advanced technical state of monastery brewing.

One of the main reasons for the rapid expansion of monastery breweries was the quite strict fasting rules of the various orders. Specifically, the monks soon realized that beer was more than a refreshing drink.

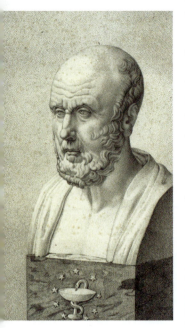

Hippocrates
(ca. 460 – 377 BC)

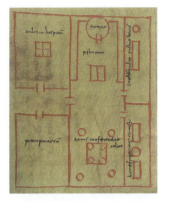

Plan of the St. Gallen monastery brewery from the year 840. Separate brewing and storage areas for beer brewing are clearly visible.

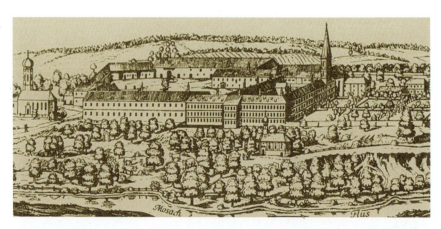

The Weihenstephan Monastery near Munich.

If it is brewed strong enough, it can also provide a good part of the daily caloric requirement and make the long fasting periods easier to bear. The rules of the monastic orders required abstinence from food for days or sometimes weeks, only drink was allowed in keeping with the church's maxim: "liquida non frangunt ieunum"—liquids do not break the fast.

The misleading term "liquid bread" originates from this time, and in this simple, abbreviated form it no longer applies to beer, as we shall see.

The monasteries soon developed their own beer culture, and monastery beer was of better quality than beers brewed in the surrounding area. Inventive monks soon recognized that selling beer was a way of tapping an interesting source of revenue for the monastery. But the monasteries weren't the only ones to realize this. Emperors, kings, and princes also benefited from issuing brewing rights—and of course from the taxing of beer brewing.

Monasteries which had been issued brewing rights were able to operate like commercial breweries and compete with secular beer makers. Compared to them, however, they had not inconsiderable competitive advantages. They had cheap grain from their own fields, income from donations and tithes, and almost free labor. They were also exempt from paying taxes and were never affected by brewing bans. Such bans were issued by the authorities during poor harvests in order to secure grain for the vital production of bread for the population.

Monasteries were exempt from taxes and brewing bans.

One of the most important monastery breweries was and is the Weihenstephan Monastery near Munich, which was granted the right to brew in 1146. It is one of the oldest surviving breweries in the world. The Munich University of Technology's faculty of brewing has been located there since 1930. The monks in Weihenstephan became aware of the importance of hops in brewing in 1150. Their hop fields are located between Inn, Alz and Salzach, in the Salzburger Land, in Upper and Lower Austria, in Carinthia and in Tyrol.

The Purity Law of 1516

In order to protect the health of the population, princes and rulers frequently found themselves compelled to issue strict ordinances against the adulteration of beer. For the beer drunk in the middle Ages had almost nothing in common with what we understand as beer today. In addition to barley, its ingredients included wheat, oats, millet, beans, peas, and other starchy grains. It is known that hops were not added to the wort until the late Middle Ages, although it had been grown as a cultivated plant since the 8th century.

Special stamp issued by the German Post Office: 450 years of the German Purity Law for beer.

Wie das Pier summer vñ winter auf dem Land sol geschenckt vnd prauen werden

Item Wir ordnen/setzen/vnnd wöllen/ mit Rathe vnnser Lanndtschafft / das füran allennthalben in dem Fürstenthůmb Bayrñ/auff dem lande/ auch in vnsern Stettñ vñ Märckthen/da deßhalb hieuor kain sonndere ordnung ist / von Michaelis biß auff Georij/ ain maß oder kopffpiers über ainen pfenning Müncher werung/ vñ von sant Jorgen tag/biß auff Michaelis/ die maß über zwen pfenning derselben werung / vnd der enden der kopff ist / über drey haller/bey nachgesetzter Pene/nicht gegeben noch außgeschenckht sol werden. Wo auch ainer nit Mertzñ / sonder annder Pier prawen/oder sonst haben würde/sol Er d och das/kains wegs höher/dann die maß vmb ainen pfenning schencken/vnd verkauffen. Wir wöllen auch sonderlichen/ das füran allenthalben in vnsern Stetten/Märckthen/ vñ auff dem Lannde/ zů kainem Pier/merer stück/ dañ allain Gersten /Hopffen/vñ wasser/ genomen vñ geprauche sölle werdñ. Welher aber dise vnsere Ordnung wissentlich überfaren vnnd nit hallten wurde / dem sol von seiner gerichtzöbrigkait/ dasselbig vas Pier/zůstraff vnnachläßlich/ so offt es geschicht / genommen werden. Jedoch wo ain Grůwirt von ainem Pierprewen in vnnsern Stettñ/ Märckten/oder aufm lande/yezůzeitñ ainen Emer piers/ zwen oder drey/kauffen / vnd wider vnnter den gemaynnen Pawrsuolck außschenncken würde/ dem selben allain/ aber sonnßt nyemandts/sol dye maß/ oder der kopffpiers/ vmb ainen haller höher dann oben gesetzt ist/ zegeben/ vñ/ außzeschencken erlaubt vnnd vnuerpotñ.

The use of such strange-sounding additives as pitch, ox gall, horse-heal, eggs, soot, and chalk, in addition to many spices, medicinal herbs, and hemp from the monastery gardens, led Prince Wilhelm IV of Bavaria to issue a "purity law" on 23 April 1516. It survives to this day in Germany's Beer Tax Law as the "German Purity Law."

It is less well known that the city of Augsburg implemented a similar regulation about 100 years before the purity law. This regulation stated that only water, barley malt, and hops could be used in the making of beer. The existence of the fourth ingredient, beer yeast, was unknown at that time, as yeast cells can only be seen under a microscope with a magnification factor of 800. But all rules have their exceptions. Made from wheat malt, the popular *Weißbier* from Bavaria was exempted from this regulation, whereby the German princes secured a monopoly for the brewing of these wheat beers and for centuries secured for themselves a not unattractive source of income. But the Purity Law was also enacted under "gentle" pressure from church authorities. As we saw above, considerable quantities of beer were consumed in the monasteries, both by the monks and the nuns. The most commonly-used flavoring ingredient was hemp, a relative of the hop plant, whose slightly aphrodisiac, stimulating effect was not exactly conducive to a monastic, celibate life.

The components of hops have an antiseptic effect.

The soothing, soporific effect of hops, on the other hand, was more compliant with spirituality, and therefore one could characterize the Purity Law as one of the world's first "drug laws."

In the Middle Ages, the brewing of beer was largely reliant on wild yeasts present in the ambient air. It is not difficult to imagine that this often resulted in faulty fermentation and taste deficiencies. Despite everything, however, at that time beer was by far the most hygienic and digestible beverage available to the consumer. Because of the absence of sanitary facilities in the cities, milk and water were contaminated with germs and bacteria. In contrast, the beer wort was at least boiled with hops and thus sterilized. Admittedly no one then knew that hops and its contents had an antiseptic effect. Doctors and scientists, such as Paracelsus (1493–1541), already suspected these connections.

In a scientifically unenlightened time, in the Middle Ages many beer brewers came under "suspicion of casting spells." Beer did unite the four elements: water in the brewing water, grain for earth, air in fermentation, and fire in the brewing process. Brewing turned a solid material—grain—into a new product—liquid beer, an incomprehensible alchemistic process to the uneducated laymen!

Paracelsus (1493–1541). (Photo: Levity.com)

Vienna Style Lager Beer

*In the ice house.
(Photo: Franz Reil)*

The next great step in the development of brewing took place in the middle of the 19th century. The invention of the first electric refrigeration system by Carl von Linde (1842–1934) in 1870 made it possible for bottom-fermented beer, which has a longer shelf life, to be brewed all year long.

Until then it was only possible to produce bottom-fermented beer during the colder months of the year. Ice was "harvested" with great effort from ice ponds and glaciers in winter and then stored in the breweries' so-called ice cellars.

The name "*Märzenbier*" (March beer) dates back to this era, for before the invention of electric refrigeration, bottom-fermented beers—which require a temperature below 10° C for fermentation—could only be brewed roughly into the month of March in Central Europe. The use of electric refrigeration made it possible to produce longer-lasting beer, which could be transported, all year long regardless of the external weather influences. The new methods of transportation, such as railroads and steam ships, then accelerated the development and spread of branded beers, which previously had been brewed for local consumption. But it also began the process of concentration in brewing, which is still not finished. Meanwhile, a few global brewing concerns dominate the brewing market with standard beer types, which must always taste the same and which are supposed to be and are interchangeable. With pasteurization for preservation and mechanical

The first Linde refrigeration machine. (Photo: Vienna Technical Museum)

filtering of yeast components from the beer using diatomaceous earth filters, the step from food to beverage was completed. This globalization process has eliminated any of the elements previously found naturally in beer, such as B-complex vitamins in the yeast.

Another milestone in the development of modern beers was the discovery of yeast as the cause of alcoholic fermentation and its reproduction in pure culture. With these yeast strains from the laboratory, which are always available in consistent quality and which breweries even protect with patents, it has become possible to produce beer of standardized, consistent quality.

> Whereas mainly dark top-fermented beers, which have a short shelf life and are not suitable for storage, were produced into the 19th century, with the development of a new brewing method by the Austrian Anton Dreher in 1841, the lager beer from Klein-Schwechat near Vienna began its triumphal march around the entire world.

In the millennia from the Sumerians to the present day, nothing permanently changed, indeed revolutionized, the making of beer as did Anton Dreher's "lager beer." This pale, bottom-fermented beer, which differed clearly from the cloudy, dark beers of the competition, was enthusiastically welcomed by consumers. By way of Pilsen and Budweis, the Czech beer centers then part of the Danube Monarchy, the method made its way to Munich, was constantly refined, scientifically analyzed by the technical university, and developed further. Today, the vast majority of the beers brewed worldwide are produced using the method developed by Anton Dreher.

Anton Dreher.

Another important step toward a new beer culture was the development of glass bottles at the end of the 19th century, first with the swing-top and porcelain cap, followed by the crown cap with indents, which are also used today. For the first time it was possible not just to drink beer in public houses or consume beer made at home, but to buy it ahead and drink it within one's own four walls. Today in Europe standardized Euro returnable bottles are used for beer. Refillable, they are more environmentally-friendly. Increasingly, however, designers are coming up with bottles and glasses for the various beer types. In recent years, so-called NRW bottles, which are somewhat taller and slimmer, have become popular. According to the manufacturers they have less air in the bottle neck, resulting in reduced risk of impurities and longer-lasting beer.

Modern breweries resemble huge industrial complexes with smokestacks, laboratories, fermentation tanks, lagering cellars, and bottling facilities, which produce beer in a computer-assisted industrial process. In-house laboratories and attending inspections ensure consistent quality of the barley malt.

Unfortunately many beneficial contents of the beer are lost as a result of this process. Modern filtering systems in the breweries filter out the last remaining components of the yeast after fermentation.

The "pure" pale beers have a longer shelf life as a result of this process and are less susceptible to flavor changes. Lacking nourishment in the form of sugar, after fermentation the living microorganisms in the yeast die, settle on the bottom of the bottle as sediment, and as they decompose can negatively affect the flavor of the beer. The reverse side of the coin is, of course, that many of the components of the beer yeast, like vitamins and trace minerals, and the contents of the hops are also removed from the finished beer. The same applies to pasteurization, in which the beer is briefly heated to 72° C after bottling. This kills possible contaminants in the bottles which might lead to undesirable noxious fermentation. These processes turn a "living" staple food into a more or less "dead" beverage, however. It is argued that the consumer and especially the marketing channels by way of supermarkets and gas stations, where beer cannot always be stored under optimal temperatures and light conditions, demand a product best suited to these storage environments.

Beer pub with micro brewery.

As a result of this worldwide concentration process in brewing, the many local or regional breweries, which usually supplied beer for one town or even for their own pubs, have disappeared, or the smaller brands have been swallowed up by the bigger brewing companies. With this the diversity of types and flavors of beer has unfortunately been lost.

These brewing concerns that dominate the market are of course a not insignificant economic factor with their advertising in the media, as sponsors of major sporting events, and as employers. On the other hand there are still many mid-size and small breweries, which are able to score in the regional and local spheres with special beers. With respect to prices, however, these small breweries are fighting a hopeless battle against the big companies. But most of the innovative beers, combined with traditional brewing skill, which result in amazing taste experiences, come from the small breweries, which regard beer making as craftsmanship and not as an industrial manufacturing process.

Small tavern brewing system.

In Germany, only in Bavaria, particularly in Franconia, are numerous small breweries which supply just a few inns able to survive. The late 1980s and early 1990s saw the beginning of a counter-movement—late, almost too late, for many of these traditional small breweries. Once again there are public house breweries and lost and forgotten beer specialties are again being brewed according to the old recipes and warmly received by beer lovers.

This development has also resulted in the rise of a corresponding beer culture. Whereas some time ago it was almost impossible or nearly unthinkable to order a beer with a meal in a fine restaurant, today restaurants have extensive beer lists, analogous to wine lists, from which customers can select a beer to accompany their meal. And a fine pilsner is now offered as a selection alongside all the other aperitifs.

The big international brewing concerns are always on the lookout for new beer creations that can revive the relatively saturated mass market in Europe with new beers and thus separate themselves from their competitors. This process began several years ago with mixed beers such as Radler—beer and lemonade—and similar products. Corn-based beers from Mexico were imported or brewed under license. Drunk from the bottle with a slice of lime, they appealed to a new and mainly youthful public. So-called "ice beers," almost frozen and again drunk from the bottle, have also become trendy in recent years. This constant search for new beer creations has led to new types of beer, some with hemp or chili pods replacing hops. Most new developments and experiments with new flavor nuances are surely coming from the USA and Canada, where additives and substitute ingredients unimaginable in Central European terms, are used in home and craft brewing.

Raw Materials for the Brewing of Beer

Beer is a carbonated, lightly-alcoholic beverage made of water, hops, and malt and fermented by yeast. The variety of beers that can be made by slight variations in these ingredients is actually surprising. In Central Europe the allowable ingredients, influenced by the "German Purity Law," have changed little, while in other countries, particularly overseas, other ingredients have become accepted as ingredients.

> For cost reasons, expensive malt has in some cases been replaced by much cheaper starch-containing cereals, in particular rice, wheat, and corn, which are added in the form of unmalted adjuncts.

The enzyme in the malted barley then breaks down these starchy grains during the brewing process. In addition to wheat, fruit is used in the making of specialty beers, especially in Belgium, France, and the Netherlands. Cherries, raspberries, and other similar fruits are used. Chemical additives, to stabilize the head, and chemical preservatives are also scorned by European beer makers. These chemical and, therefore, artificial additives are neither needed nor advisable for home brewing.

Water

Hops

Brewing Malt

Additives and Spices

Beer Yeast

Finished home brewing mixes, usually in dehydrated form, are common in Great Britain. They need only the addition of water for fermentation and produce a "beer-like" beverage.

Complete packages are sold as "beer kits."

It is the goal of this book to get away from these "instant beverages" in favor of self-brewed beers made from hops, water, and malt. These home brew mixes are offered as "beer kits," which range from complete mixtures with hops to semi-complete products which contain only liquid malt extract. A not inconsiderable amount of sugar is also required in order to ensure proper fermentation.

Obviously there are specialty beers which use special additives, such as the Trappist beers in Belgium and Holland, which are post-fermented in the bottle using candy sugar, or Geuze which—like champagne—is a blend of various old beer types in a champagne-like bottle sealed with a cork.

The same goes for home brewing: to produce a natural product using natural raw materials and natural processes.

When brewing at home, one should keep in mind that beer brewing is applied biotechnology. The overriding principle should be to produce a natural beverage without chemical additives using natural materials and natural processes. Because of the quantities of beer made in home brewing there will, of course, always be differences in flavor, regardless of the ingredients used, therefore you will find it difficult to make the exact same beer twice in a row.

It is precisely this diversity and the individual deviations in flavor that make home brewing so interesting and fascinating.

As with all activities, in beer brewing, too, practice makes perfect. Therefore don't allow failures to discourage you from trying again. We strongly recommend that you keep a brewing log so that you can use the lessons of experience in future (you will find a template for such a brewing log on page 96).

Water

The most important raw material in beer making is water, which accounts for 90% of the finished product. The quality of the beer largely depends on the quality and composition of the brewing water.

It is therefore no coincidence that—despite ignorance of this fact and without extensive chemical analysis of the water—there were and still are particularly good beers in many areas.

An example of this is the original pilsner from Pilsen, which is world famous and whose good reputation is almost solely due to the excellent soft water of Bohemia. With the help of the latest chemical analysis, it is now possible to determine the precise composition of brewing water and prepare it for brewing purposes prior to brewing using various physical and chemical processes. For only with suitable water in sufficient quantities can one brew good beer. The breweries know the importance of brewing water in the making of beer and therefore spare no expense or effort to prepare water for their brewing purposes. The breweries use filtration, water-softening systems, gypsum, dissolved and undissolved chalk and phosphate eliminators (ion exchangers) to give the water the necessary hardness for each particular beer before brewing.

Nowadays, one can use a wide variety of physical and chemical processes to prepare water for brewing purposes.

Degree of Hardness of Brewing Water

Brewing water should be as soft as possible—not more than 100 mg CaO/l—and as free as possible of nitrates, magnesium, sulfur and other, especially organic, impurities.

Pure, soft water is an essential requirement for a good beer.

On the other hand certain specialty beers, for example *Kölsch*, are
brewed using especially hard water, and this hard water gives the beer its
unique flavor. Brewing water's degree of hardness depends on its content of
salts, minerals, and trace elements, which are naturally absorbed from the
earth. The total hardness of the water consists of the carbonate hardness and
the non-carbonate hardness. Carbonate hardness is particularly important
in home brewing, non-carbonate hardness less so.

Hard brewing water requires significantly less hops, otherwise the beer
will be bitter and have an unpleasant obtrusive hop taste. Pilsner beers,
which are brewed using extremely soft water, can endure significantly larger
hop additions without the bitter substances in the hops becoming obtrusive.

Dark beers are for the most part brewed with hard water and contain
less hops than pale beers. The individual flavor of the beer depends
on the qualities of the brewing water, which is largely responsible for
the respective beer quality.

During brewing, the water salts in hard water combine with the soluble
elements in the malt and hops and negatively affect the work of the enzymes
in the malt. Given the same materials—hard water results in rather darker
beer, while soft water tends to produce paler beers. Also, hard water results
in a significantly lower yield per brew, therefore breweries usually soften their
water to a value of 20 to 50 mg CaO/l in order to survive in the competitive
marketplace.

If your water is too hard for the type of beer you are planning to brew,
you have several options for treating the water. As previously mentioned,
carbonate hardness, in particular, influences brewing results negatively, and
this can be dealt with by boiling the water before brewing. After some time
the chalk precipitates from the water and settles on the bottom of the pot as
sediment. This chalk or scale is also undesirable for cooking in the kitchen.
After cooling the water, carefully siphon it from the pot, leaving behind the
sediment. Taking into account evaporation and wastage, you will need 25
to 30 liters of brewing water for about 20 liters of beer, and a considerable
expenditure of energy is required.

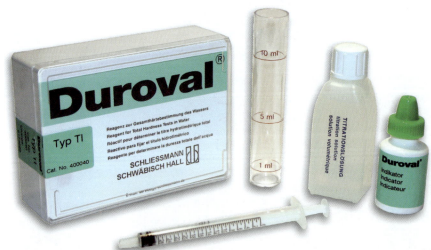

Photo: www.holzeis.com

If the brew water has more than 100 mg CaO/l, another simple chemical form of brew water preparation is to add common gypsum. You will need about 1 tablespoon of gypsum for 10 liters of brewing water. It is dissolved and added to the brew water while stirring. Afterwards the brewing water is again carefully siphoned off, leaving the sediment in the pot. It is also possible to add dissolved or undissolved chalk to the water in the manner just described. These methods require a certain amount of scientific knowledge and, as powerful chemical reactions with corrosive spatters and corresponding heat generation involve a certain amount of risk, the chemical treatment of brewing water should be the final alternative for the home brewer. In addition to the classic hobby brewer methods of boiling or mixing with distilled water, someone who wishes to prepare his own well water simply and effectively can turn to good old Cadurex®. A simple device for softening water, whose catalyst (Lewatit) is even recyclable. To begin with, one can and will get by with the available water and try to brew beers with its degree of hardness. After all there are, as mentioned, beers that are produced with extremely hard water.

> **BY THE WAY:**
>
> The chlorine possibly added to the water by your local treatment plant escapes during boiling or during the brewing process. More worrying, however, is contamination of the water with nitrates and nitrites from agriculture. This qualitative impairment affects most drinking water.

The pH Value of the Brewing Water

The pH value (acid value) of the brewing water should not be greater than 5, for at such levels the breakdown of starch and protein by the enzymes in the malt is not as complete as at lower pH values. This pH value has a crucial effect on the activity of the enzymes and thus the yield of the brew. For the hobby brewer the simplest way of dealing with high pH is biological acidification, for example using food-safe lactic acid to reduce pH to a desirable level. On the other hand, excessive treatment of the brewing water at home is not advised, for this means interfering with the natural raw material that comprises the greatest part of the final product—the finished beer. As well, from an economic point of view, a small improvement in batch yield is not as important to you as it is to a large brewery, which is in competition with other breweries and therefore must exploit every competitive advantage.

The pH value of water has a significant effect on the activity of enzymes.

You can inquire about the degree of hardness of your water at your local water works, where they can also advise you of the water's pH value. You can also check the pH level of the water yourself using simple, commercially available pH test strips. Simply hold a test strip in the selected brewing water and then compare the color of the test strip with the scale on the container. If your local water is too polluted for brewing purposes, you can also use bottled water or mineral water (non-carbonated) for home brewing, which of course will drive up the cost of your beer.

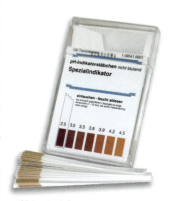

pH test strips.

For brewing, both at home and commercially, water is not only used as a raw material with which to make beer. Several times as much is used for cooling and especially cleaning, for in making beer cleanliness is the top priority and for this hygienically perfect water is needed.

The breweries appreciate the importance of optimal brewing water and spare no cost and effort to ensure that this vital raw material is always available in sufficient quantities with consistent quality.

Hops

Hop is a climbing plant related to hemp, which is grown as a field crop in hop gardens. The hop plants climb along hop posts or hop wires, reaching heights of up to eight meters. During the growth phase hops grow approximately 15 centimeters per day. It is found in wild form beside streams, in the forest, and in hedges, where it is a parasitic plant, using trees and shrubs as host plants.

Unfertilized female flower clusters are mainly used for the making of beer, although some English beers are brewed with the male umbels of the hop (additional information may be found in the descriptions of these special beers).

The components of hops, the so-called lupulin seeds, contain bitter-tasting substances which give beer its characteristic flavor and acridness.

While the proportion of hops in finished beer, depending on the type, is relatively low at about 200 to 500 grams per hectoliter. Without this characteristic bitter tone of the hops beer, as the refreshing drink we imagine it today, would not taste like beer. The Babylonians and Egyptians used hops in making their beer; the early Germans, however, used bitter oak bark even though they were familiar with the hop as a cultivated plant and ate the hop tips as a vegetable similar to asparagus—a tradition that continues to the present day in Belgium.

Whereas in the past the hop was mainly used to make beer durable, without the knowledge that the contents of the hop have an antibacterial effect, today the hop is used in beer making mainly for its fine, bitter taste.

A hop field. (Photo: Austrian Brewing Association)

Of particular importance, however, is one quality of the hop that is used in brewing—its role in breaking down proteins—during boiling of the wort.

Boiling causes proteins to leave the wort. It is later filtered out of the wort as hot or cold sediment or pumped out in a so-called whirlpool.

Hop Varieties

Basically two kinds of hops are used in brewing, bittering hops and the higher quality, and also more expensive, aroma hops, which are used in pilsner-style beers, the most commonly brewed bottom-fermented types made today.

Entire regions are known for the production of hops, for example Hallertau, Spalt, and the area around Tettnang in Bavaria, and Saaz in the Czech Republic with its world-famous aroma hops for pilsner beers.

During the making of beer, hops help in the removal of proteins and the addition of hops reduces physically-related cloudiness in the beer. It also has a positive effect on the consistency of the head and its stabilizing effect gives the beer a longer shelf life. All of the active substances and ingredients of hops have not yet been fully analyzed and researched.

Dried cone hops.
(Photo: www.holzeis.com)

Hops for brewing come in a wide variety of forms, from dried hop flowers, hop powder in cans or in so-called pellets (small compressed sticks, roughly the thickness of cigarettes) to liquid hop extract.

> Which of these processed forms of hops you choose to use for making beer is not that crucial; of greater importance is the quality of the natural hops from which the completed product is made.

There are significant differences in aroma and bittering substances depending on the variety and year. The essential oils of the hop are highly volatile. Consequently, optimal storage of this agricultural product at the correct temperature (in a refrigerator) and humidity is particularly important. If stored incorrectly, hops lose up to 35% of their brewing value in a single year, as their delicate aromic substances are lost. The best place to store hops for home brewing is therefore in the vegetable compartment of the refrigerator. Hop pellets can also be kept frozen.

Hop pellets.

The Addition of Hops

Use caution when adding hops to the wort! The correct dosing of hops requires a great deal of skill and, above all, experience.

> ### BASIC RULE:
>
> The more hops, the bitterer the beer; the less hops, the milder and maltier it tastes. As so often in life, here too: "The proof of the pudding is in the eating"!

The supplier of your hops will surely provide you with a product description, or a brewmaster will give you information about the quality and, above all, the intensity of the hops used. For example, the dried, pressed hops, pressed hop pellets, and hop powder concentrate are significantly more intensive than dried natural hops in cone form. The intensity of the bitter substance of the hop (alpha acid content) is given in standardized form as BE (bitter units) or IBU (International Bittering Units). Hop varieties with a wide variety of bittering units are used depending on the type of beer. The recipes in this book include the appropriate bitter units.

Dried natural hops and hop pellets.

> ## ATTENTION!
>
> Try to experiment with medium strength hop varieties first and find out which appeal to you.

In the subsequent recipes section we always assume the use of hop pellets, as these are much easier to measure out and weigh than dried natural hops. Also, hop pellets can be purchased vacuum-packed in small quantities and are thus easier to store at home. These create less residue during filtering and simplify the filtering process, whereas dried hop leaves easily clog the filter cloth during filtering of the wort. With natural hops it is possible to add them to the wort in packets—similar to teabags—which simplifies filtering.

High-quality aroma hops are most often used in making pilsner-style beers, with their marked bitter flavor. Various other types are used in beers with a more malty character. Each brewmaster uses mixtures of various hop varieties to brew his own flavor of beer. But the quality—and once again especially the hardness—of the brewing water affects the selection and quantity of hops. Calciferous, hard water for example enhances the bitter substances of the hop; consequently, the brewer needs less during brewing. There is a risk, however, that the beer will not have a "round" flavor and the desired bitterness of the hops will become intrusive.

The hops are not added all at once during the boiling of the wort; instead, the so-called hop dosage is divided into as many as five additions, with the highest quality and most expensive hop varieties not being added to the wort until the end of the boiling process.

Addition of hops to the wort.

Of course, quality comes at a price. Even if only about 20% of the hop bittering substances remain in the finished product, it would be wrong to skimp on quality here. The hop oils give the beer its aroma and the tannins have a positive effect on the shelf life and durability of the finished beer. The antiseptic effect of the lupulin seeds, which prevent the reproduction of lactic acid bacteria, is also not insignificant in the making of beer. On the other hand special lactic acid cultures are intentionally added to some kinds of beer, *Berliner Weisse* and Belgian special beers for example, to enrich the variety of flavors, something feared by brewers for millennia, as these unwanted lactic acid bacteria render the beer sour and unenjoyable.

Brewing Malt

The second most important raw material by volume after water is the brewing malt, which is largely made from two-row summer barley (malting barley).

This malting barley differs from feed barley in having more starch, which the enzymes in the malting barley convert into maltose (malt sugar).

Feed barley on the other hand contains less starch but more protein and is thus better for the feeding of animals. For certain special beers unmalted malting barley or wheat is used as a so-called grain adjunct.

The malting barley is processed into malt through the malting process, in which it is brought to sprouting through the addition of water and then kilned (dried) at temperatures between 70 and 100° C. When malt is spoken of in this book it basically means barley malt. Many specialty beers, especially those not subject to the tradition of the German Purity Law, use other kinds of malt such as wheat, rye, spelt, and other varieties of grain, either malted or unmalted as a grain adjunct.

Malting barley.

For economic reasons cheaper substitutes, such as rice or corn, are added to the barley malt, whereby the enzymes in the barley malt break down these adjuncts into sugar.

Maltose and dextrin (simple sugars) are those components of the malt that develop from the protein in the malt, then find themselves in the end product beer (converted into alcohol and carbon dioxide). They are reputedly responsible for beer's proverbial nutritiousness, something Saint Hildegard von Bingen knew in the Middle Ages.

The breakdown of starch in the malt is made possible by two different enzymes: alpha-amylase and beta-amylase, which work at different temperatures.

Hildegard von Bingen.

Malting barley during the malting process.

Enzymes are biocatalysts which are produced in living cells and initiate or accelerate biochemical processes, in which the enzymes themselves remain unchanged. One can therefore simply say that beer comes from fermented sugar water and that the biochemical process that takes place has remained unchanged for millennia. Well-malted malt contains many enzymes which become active at different temperatures during the brewing process and then convert the sugar in the malting barley into sugar (maltose and dextrin). Good brewing malt contains between 60 and 80% starch, along with mineral trace elements such as phosphates, silicic acid, potassium, iron, and sulfur, which are important components of finished beer.

Malt Varieties

Around the world, malt for the making of beer is produced from more than 300 different varieties of malting barley. The variety of flavors that can be achieved through variations of these malting barley varieties, some of which are grown for the breweries by contract farmers, is amazing. The home brewer can choose from a wide selection of different varieties offered by brew shops. As well, there are prepared mixed malt varieties for special beers, especially English and American beers.

There are ready-made malt mixes for specialty beers.

Even today brewers name brewing malts after their places of origin. For example, a "Vienna style" malt is better suited for making pale beers, whereas a "Munich malt" produces a darker beer for the same quantity of malt.

In our recipes you will usually also find a precise type designation in brackets beside the designation pale malt, which you can obtain from mail order stores under the same name. In addition to the designations "pilsner" and "Vienna malt," a categorization of the color intensity of brewing malt by the EBC (European Brewery Convention) has caught on—similar to the standardization of the bittering substances of hops. Pilsner malt has an EBC designation of 2-3, Vienna malt 5-8, Munich malt 12-25 and roasted malts, which are used in concentration to affect color, 900-1500.

Malt: uncrushed, crushed pale and caramel malt.

For your first brewing attempts you can use mixtures in liquid form—so-called beer kits. We recommend that you start with this entirely usable "warm-up brewing method," which is ideally suited to so-called "basement work," and wait until later to use real malt in crushed form, if available. Crushed malt has a very short shelf life and should therefore be used immediately. Malt is available in crushed form from specialized brew shops. Malt in uncrushed form has a much longer shelf life than crushed malt, for in the latter form the enzymes become inactive after a certain time. Many of these specialized dealers offer complete malt mixtures for certain quantities; their regularly-appearing catalogues provide exact information as to quantities and prices. *It might be more economical for several hobby brewers to combine their orders for larger quantities*. Exchanging ideas with brewing colleagues will make your new hobby even more interesting.

Crushed malt may only be stored for a short time.

The Malting Process

For better understanding, the malting process will be described here in brief. In the past the malthouse was an important part of every brewery, but the malter as an occupation has since split off from that of brewer. Today only a few, mainly huge brewing concerns have their own malthouses, which also produce malt for other breweries on commission. Today malthouses are service enterprises which, on behalf of the breweries, malt the raw material provided them by the latter, the malting barley, according to their wishes and specifications.

Currently almost all varieties of malt are produced in electric malting machines using hot air, whereas earlier the malt was roasted over an open fire, which gave it its characteristic smoky flavor.

Only a few specialty beers in Franconia are still produced as "*Rauchbiere,*" using malt roasted over an open beech wood fire. In the past all beer probably had a smoky taste as the malt was all roasted over an open fire.

Sprouted barley.

The Malting Process

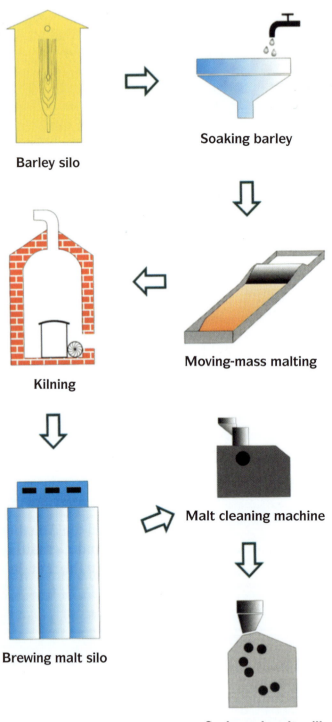

Barley silo

Soaking barley

Moving-mass malting

Kilning

Malt cleaning machine

Brewing malt silo

Scale and malt-mill

The graphic representation on page 36 illustrates the individual steps in the malting process. After a thorough cleaning, the two-row summer barley (malting barley) is mixed with water, soaked in the water for several days and then brought to germination at about 18° C. The west barley is constantly aerated to prevent it from getting moldy and germinates for about a week at 18°–20° C. It is subsequently dried at temperatures of 80°–105° C—depending on the desired malt. The barley roughly doubles in volume during this process and forms sprouts—similar to the bean sprouts seen in Chinese restaurants. This barley, which has not yet been dried or kilned, is called green malt. Light malt for the production of pale beers is dried at about 80° C. Dark malt for true dark beers, not colored beers, on the other hand is dried, or toasted, at temperatures in excess of 100° C.

As the production of brewing malt is very time-consuming and laborious, we recommend that you purchase malt for the brewing of your beer that is already in the form of finished brewing malt. Of course, if you do not shy away from the effort, you can carry out this process at home using your oven or dehydrating device used for fruit. If you do make your own brewing malt at home, however, it is better to skip the difficult and time-consuming roasting process and use untoasted green malt for your brewing attempts. This green malt has the advantage of having significantly more active enzymes than toasted malt, for inevitably some of the enzymes become inactive during the drying process. Some breweries, especially those that have their own malting houses, use a small amount of green malt in certain specialty beers.

> *Malt can be made in an oven or dehydrator.*

The only reason why green malt is not available in stores is that it is unsuitable for storage and transport and must be used immediately after germination.

For home brewing the use of green malt or a percentage of green malt is no disadvantage, as you will not be malting huge quantities of malt. If you work with unmalted grain adjuncts in your brewing experiments, this green malt is particularly suitable for breaking down the starch in the unmalted grain into sugar.

Crushing the Malt

The malt produced from the malting barley must be crushed before beginning the actual brewing process so that the individual components can better dissolve in the brewing water. Large malt mills are used for this, crushing the grain instead of turning it into flour. Malt that has not been crushed can be stored much longer than malt that has already been ground. If you have a grain mill, you should always freshly coarse-grind the required malt. Some multi-purpose kitchen machines also have attachments that allow you to crush your malt. It should be mentioned that processing the grain at home inevitably produces a certain amount of dust, therefore already ground and vacuum-packed malt is preferable to grinding it yourself. Less well suited are coffee grinders, as the grinding cannot be precisely controlled, resulting

Grain mill: suitable for crushing malt.

in malt that is ground too fine. As well, the capacity of such coffee grinders is very limited. Processing three to five kilograms of malt is usually too big a job for a coffee grinder. Very well suited for the crushing of malt kernels are machines sold in drugstores and health food stores for producing flakes from grain. Even though it takes a great deal of time to crush 3–5 kg of malt, the results are relatively satisfactory. Kitchen machines for grating nuts, and graters, either electric or manual, are partly suitable for crushing brewing malt. Special malt grinders, similar to the meat grinders or grain mills used in kitchens, are now available from specialty shops, making the use of uncrushed malt an interesting option.

> ### ATTENTION!
>
> These devices only look similar to malt mills! Inside the latter there are non-cutting roller or crushing (short grinding path) works which prevent cutting of the hulls and conversion of too much grain into flour.

Grinders similar to pepper mills are therefore to be avoided, otherwise the result will be clumping during the brewing process and poor-quality wort.

To prevent dust from forming the malt should be soaked before it is ground.

As previously mentioned, all of these methods inevitably result in the formation of a certain amount of dust, and some home brewing books recommend the grinding of pre-soaked malt. The temperature at which the malt is mixed with the water should not exceed 8–10° C in order to prevent premature activation of the enzymes in the brewing malt. The malt can easily be soaked for several hours or even overnight. Malt crushed in this way—the result is more likely a paste—must be used immediately after it is processed (mashed)! You should always soak just enough malt for the beer you are making. Note that water is, of course, used for soaking, which will influence the amount of water added during mashing. The enzymes in the malt begin working when water is added, which can lead to changes in the saccharification process.

The malt enzymes begin working as soon as water is added.

Special Malts

Caramel Malt

Specially-treated, so-called "caramel malts" are used to round out the flavor of the beer. Available in specialty shops, these malts give the beer its full-bodied taste.

These special malts are only added to the mash in small quantities (maximum addition 20% of the weight of the mash).

Select these special malts from the appropriate mail order catalogue.

Colored Malts

When brewing darker beers, colored malt, malt kilned at a higher temperature, is added to the light malt, which darkens the pale beer These colored malts should not be confused with dark malt, which is used in the brewing of darker beers.

Colored malt is kilned at high temperatures.

> To avoid these darker malts compromising taste, colored malts should not make up more than 2% of the total weight of the malt.

Nowadays many breweries no longer make their dark beers with dark malt, instead coloring them with caramel after brewing. The making of this additive, the only one permitted by the German Purity Law for the coloring of top-fermented wheat beers, will be described later (see page 43).

If caramel or colored malts are unavailable by mail order, with time and effort you can make it yourself at home in the oven using unbroken light malt. Mix 1 kg of light malt with 0.5 l of water until the water is completely absorbed by the malt. Saccharification takes place in the oven at a temperature of 64° C. The same biochemical process takes place as during mashing of the malt in brewing water. Three to four hours are necessary to saccharify the relatively large amount of malt in the oven (with the oven door closed). If you wish to make caramel malt, subsequently dry the malt at about 170-180° C, leaving the oven door open enough to allow the liquid in the malt to escape. At these temperatures, the sugar in the brewing malt caramelizes, not unlike in the described process for making caramel. This roasting process takes another roughly two hours. While the malt is roasting, sprinkle if frequently with water to make up for the fluid loss. If you wish to make colored malt, subsequently raise the temperature quickly to about 220° C. As you see, making these two kinds of malt at home is both time consuming and energy intensive.

> If you nevertheless decide to carry out this process at home, we recommend that you make both varieties of malt in one step, in a ratio of 4:1 (caramel malt to colored malt), as caramel malt is used in significantly greater quantities in brewing than colored malt is for coloring the beer.

The finished caramel or colored malt should be placed in an air-tight container and stored in a cool place, as enough is made for several batches of beer. Airtight plastic bags or glass jars with screw-on caps are suitable containers.

Green Malt

"Green malt" is the unroasted malt after germination produced during the malting process. Because of the germ buds, it is almost twice the volume of the finished product, the brewing malt. Green malt is also used by breweries in various specialty beers or when a relatively large amount of adjunct is used, as this green malt contains more enzymes and is therefore ideally suited to breaking down the starch in the adjunct into sugar. During roasting some of the enzymes are lost.

> You cannot buy this malt—an intermediate product in the making of brewing malt—as it is neither storable nor transportable.

If you wish to turn malting barley into brewing malt, you can use the green malt in your home brewing without having to go through the difficult process of drying or roasting.

Wheat Malt

Weizenbiere (wheat beers), or *Weißbiere* as they are called in Bavaria, have recently enjoyed a rise in popularity. In addition to barley malt, wheat malt is also used in their production. Wheat malt is also used as an additive in *Berliner Weiße* and many Belgian and English beer varieties. These beers are usually brewed using the original brewing method—with top-fermenting yeast.

> Wheat is used in the making of beer both in malted and unmalted form, the latter as a so-called adjunct.

This grain is the only exception and deviation from barley malt allowed by the German Purity Law for the production of top-fermented wheat beers. Mixtures of 50% wheat and barley malt are used in the making of wheat beers, for an optimal filtering effect is not possible with the use of wheat alone, which lacks glumes. The glumes in the barley malt give a natural filter during the separation of solid and liquid components of the mash.

Other Malts

This book also concerns itself with specialty beers and therefore some recipes include ingredients that are not permitted under the strict terms of the German Purity Law. Some of these grain varieties used in the making of beer have traditions thousands of years old, much longer than the use of malting barley. Here in Central Europe, beers were produced from oats, rye, spelt, emmer, millet, and other types of grains and mixtures. Some small breweries, for example the Stiftsbrauerei Schlägl in Austria, are again making a rye beer using the old recipe.

Malt can be made from a variety of grains.

As these special malts are very difficult to obtain for home brewing, because they are only produced as special products by the malting houses for the respective breweries, we recommend that you use a portion in the form of unmalted grain (adjunct) when brewing such beers or experimenting with new recipes.

These grain varieties are often available from organic farms in processed form in health food stores and drugstores. If the grain is used in unmalted form, a certain amount of barley malt must be used as the enzymes in the barley malt have to do the job of breaking down the unmalted grain. The barley malt should also be as freshly-ground as possible, for then the enzymes will be much more active. The reference previously made to the absence of glumes in wheat malt also applies here. Many of these grain varieties do not develop optimal filtering qualities, therefore a mixture with at least 50% barley malt is recommended.

Liquid Malt

Liquid malt mixtures for home brewing are sold in cans or glass jars. These syrup-like liquids (resembling honey) are also produced by the malting houses and save the home-brewer the time-consuming mashing process and subsequent lautering of the mash. So as not to give any false impressions, these malt extracts are a grain-based natural product which is condensed and made to store better. The liquid malt from the can or jar only needs to be dissolved in the brewing water and boiled with hops. These liquid malt mixtures are certainly ideal for your first brewing attempts. They do, however, limit your ability to take different taste directions when brewing. These liquid malt mixtures are somewhat expensive, but for the novice they provide a perfect entry into brewing. Very often a not inconsiderable

Liquid malt extract. (Photo: www.holzeis.com)

(Photo: www.holzeis.com)

quantity of sugar is also needed. As a result of a much improved product range, this can now be replaced by unhopped liquid malt or dry malt extract of varying composition. Many German beer brewers forced to work in "beerless" foreign countries now swear by this method so as not to "die of thirst" far from home.

> So-called "beer kits," liquid malt mixtures already containing the hops and yeast, which only need to be mixed with water, have become popular, particularly in the Anglo-American countries.

With kits, the home brewer has much less freedom to achieve different flavors. Nevertheless a true brewmaster has done his work there and brewed a real beer. Reduced in weight by heat and vacuum so that they can be transported more easily, beer kits spare the home brewer the need to process raw materials. He simply needs to replace the water and complete the process with real cellar work.

"Instant beers," however, come in bags or containers and consist of malt and hops, yeast, and other ingredients in dehydrated form, developed in the laboratory and mixed according to a formula. To the mind of the beer lover, this form of "beer making" is scarcely comprehensible and is rejected by home brewers. If you are serious about home brewing you will surely switch from these prepackaged finished products (fast food for beer making) to beer made from real malt.

The last-mentioned methods are, however, useful for making a successful beginning in an almost inexhaustible and subsequently near-natural hobby. Even if you lack technical training and skill, try to overcome you initial fears and allow yourself to get a taste of what will perhaps become a highly professionally cultivated hobby.

Malt Substitutes

In contrast to the previously-described special malts for the creation of specialty beers using malts other than barley malt, for making their bottom-fermented lager beers the large international brewing concerns also use malt substitutes which are much cheaper than the barley malt made using the expensive malting process.

The main substitutes are rice and corn, which replace about 20-25% of the barley malt in the mash. Replacement of the expensive malt with other starchy grains is largely done for cost reasons.

If you intend to use such grains in the making of beer at home, we recommend that you add small amounts of these grains (maximum 20% of the grain bill) to your mash. When heating the mash, you must pay special attention to ensure that the rice or corn does not settle onto the bottom of the brew pot. Because of their higher specific gravity, these grains have a greater tendency to sink to the bottom of the pot than the lighter brewing malt and therefore tend to burn more easily, giving the mash—and thus the finished beer—an unpleasant smoky taste. The kind of starchy grain used to make a beer has a decisive impact on its taste. Beer made from cheaper raw materials must, therefore, be of poorer in terms of quality. Like malting barley, rice and corn are natural products. There are excellent rice beers, and as the success of Corona, a Mexican corn-based beer, shows, such specialty beers can even be seen as cultural drinks even if they in no way follow Central European brewing tradition.

As mentioned elsewhere, beer is essentially nothing more than fermented sugar water, therefore beet or cane sugar can partially replace malt. Especially in the English and American literature, where there are countless home brewing books, almost every recipe contains a not insignificant amount of sugar as an ingredient for the fermentation of beer. With the exception of specialty beers, for example the Trappist beers, which is fermented a second time in the bottle using candy sugar, we have consciously avoided the adding of sugar in our recipes.

Trappist beers are undergo secondary fermentation in the bottle using candy sugar.

If you nevertheless want to use sugar in brewing your beer, add it during mashing to achieve a better mixing with the malt sugar formed from the brewing malt.

Sugar is of course significantly cheaper than malt sugar, which is very expensive to produce. Note that the addition of sugar can cause the specific gravity of the wort to rise sharply. Use of a beer hydrometer to accurately measure and adjust the specific gravity of the wort is therefore indispensible.

Sugar and Sugar Color

As mentioned above, sugar could theoretically replace the malt or part of the malt; but many of the components of beer are linked to the brewing malt and pure sugar water would, if allowed to ferment, have neither the color nor the taste of beer.

The contents of beer are dependent on the brewing malt.

Caramel made from sugar can, however, be used to color beer. It makes the beer darker depending on the quantity used.

True dark beers, on the other hand, are brewed using dark malt and not colored afterwards with caramel.

You can easily make caramel yourself for home brewing. Granulated sugar is heated in a pan over medium heat until it liquefies and begins to turn brown. Constant stirring prevents the sticky mixture from burning. Water is subsequently added to this syrupy mixture, which smells like caramel candy.

Caramel is added depending on the desired color of the finished beer.

ATTENTION!

Stir constantly, otherwise the sugar will caramelize and become hard!

Depending on the desired color of the finished beer, an appropriate quantity of the caramel mixture is added to the wort during the boil with the hops. The caramel mixture can be kept for several weeks in the refrigerator in a well-sealed jar and used for later brews.

This coloring with caramel is permissible under the strict terms of the German Purity Law. Sugar, in particular candy sugar, is also used for bottle fermentation of Belgian and Dutch Trappist beers. After the primary fermentation, when the bottles are filled, a small amount of candy sugar is added. This results in a second fermentation in the bottle, which rounds out the flavor of the beer. This procedure resembles the method used in the making of champagne.

Additives and Spices

Wormwood.

Juniper.

Whereas in the Middle Ages, before the German Purity Law, beer contained all sorts of additives and spices—some of them most adventurous by current standards—to make the beer at all pleasant to drink or to cover the taste of spoiled, sour beer, today spices are only used in various specialty beers.

The pioneers in the field of adding spices to beer are the Belgians and Britons, who add coriander or juniper or dried orange peel as flavoring ingredients when brewing beer. Though not used in the brewing process, it is not uncommon in Germany for woodruff or raspberry juice to be added to beer before it is drunk, *Berliner Weiße* being one example. This results in an obvious tinting of the beer (either green or red). Even the Bavarians round off their beloved *Weißbier*, especially *Kristallweizen*, the filtered, clear version, with a slice of lemon.

So-called Radler, originally a mixture of beer and alcohol-free lemonade, is gaining popularity among young people and athletes, and several varieties are now sold premixed in bottles.

Another specialty, especially in Belgium, France, and Holland, is fruit beer, in which cherries, raspberries, or strawberries are added to the mash. This gives the beer an unusual, slightly sour taste.

With all of these additives one must differentiate between those that are added during the brewing process and those that are added afterwards, which is usually referred to as cutting the beer. When brewing at home, there are no limits to your imagination and creativity, even though some purists will scorn such beer creations. Particularly in America, the hobby brewers, organized into countless brewing clubs, are not shy about experimenting with a wide variety of additives. In addition to sugary fruits like bananas and pineapple, beer is brewed with maple syrup and honey. From vanilla pods to chili pods, every conceivable kind of spice and herb is used to supplement or even replace hops. Where the line is to be drawn here is difficult to say, for, in fact, there is nothing wrong with using natural additives. A cinnamon beer before Christmas can be a taste treat—why not?!

It should go without saying that no chemical additives, head builders, or flavor enhancers should be used in brewing beer.

While the law makes this rule the highest priority for production of a healthy food—and beer may be seen as such—by the professional breweries, it should be even more applicable to you, the home brewer. You are at the same time the producer of your home brew as well as host and consumer.

Chili can also give beer an interesting taste.

Chemical Additives

Unfortunately many food laws in Europe permit the use of chemical additives to extend the shelf life of beer or to stabilize the beer foam. Examples of this are Austria's *Codex Alimentarius Austriacus* and the German and Swiss food laws. Regrettably the overwhelming majority of industrially produced beers are pasteurized (heated to more than 72° C) for better storage and transportability. Because of this, a "food" with living elements such as yeast becomes a dead beverage, losing many of its individual taste nuances in the process. In most cases, chemical additives are not available to the home brewer, long-distance transport of your beer is not necessary, and under normal conditions a shelf life of about eight weeks should suffice to consume your production of 10-20 liters of beer.

The majority of commercially-made beer is pasteurized.

When cleaning brew pots, fermentation containers and bottles, make sure that no cleaning residue remains.

Never use normal dishwashing detergent! On one hand these detergents, which usually contain surfactants or fatty materials, decrease the surface tension of the water, preventing the beer from forming a proper, lasting head, while on the other traces of these chemical substances (such as perfumes) can remain in the beer. After cleaning, therefore, rinse your bottles with hot and then cold water.

Detergents containing surfactants or fat affect the surface tension of water.

Beer Yeast

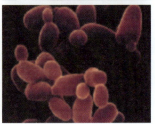

Beer yeast under the microscope.

Beer yeast breaks down the sugar formed from the brew malt into alcohol and carbon dioxide. This biochemical process is called alcoholic fermentation (correctly primary alcoholic fermentation), and the process is the same as in making wine, fruit wine, and other slightly-alcoholic drinks such as cider and mead. The yeasts used for beer making are microorganisms, which only become visible under a microscope at 800-times magnification. The process of alcoholic fermentation has not changed in thousands of years, but it was not until about 200 years ago that the invention of the microscope made it possible to attribute these processes to these microorganisms. Since the 19th century, these yeasts have been bred and multiplied into pure cultures for the making of beer.

For thousands of years "wild yeasts" were relied upon as the initiator of alcoholic fermentation in the making of beer. These wild yeasts, which are still present in the air today, can trigger undesired fermentation, although in some cases they are intentionally used to produce very special beers, such as the Belgian lambic beers.

Yeast Types

Basically two different kinds of yeast are used in beer-making, with a marked difference in their fermentation temperatures.

Bottom-fermenting yeasts (Saccaromyces carlsbergensis), which work at a fermentation temperature of 5-10° C, and top-fermenting yeasts (Saccaromyces cerevisiae), which work at a fermentation temperature of 15-20° C.

Bottom-fermenting yeast was overwhelmingly used in the making of beer until the invention of electric refrigeration by the German Carl von Linde. Previously the lower temperatures needed for the fermentation of bottom-fermented beers usually could not be achieved all year long or at best at great cost and effort. Natural ice was used for cooling. Harvested from frozen ponds near the brewery, during the winter months it was stored in huge ice cellars. This process was very expensive, as it was accomplished by a great deal of manual labor. Incidentally the name "*Märzenbier*" (March beer) originates from that time, when the month of March provided the latest opportunity to produce longer-lasting bottom-fermented beer without artificial refrigeration. Not until the invention of electric refrigeration was it possible to make bottom-fermented beers regardless of the time of year. Today, far more than 80% of all beer produced is made with bottom-fermenting yeast, as this beer is easier to transport and, more importantly, has a longer shelf life. Top-fermented beers are primarily brewed as specialty beers, which differ widely in Germany. While in England top-fermented yeasts are used to make ale, stout, and porter, in Germany these yeasts are mainly used to make *Weißbiere* (wheat beers), *Alt*, *Kölsch* and *Berliner Weiße*.

> This book has set itself the task of focusing on these specialty beers, therefore the recipe collection contains an enhanced number of these beer types made with top-fermenting yeasts.

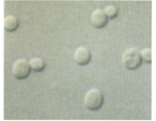

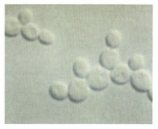

Bottom-fermenting yeast (Saccaromyces carlsbergensis) (above), top-fermenting yeast (Saccaromyces cerevisiae) (below).

The second reason why we use these top-fermenting yeasts for home brewing is purely technical. Fermentation temperatures of 15-20° C are easier to achieve and maintain at home without the need for special equipment, whereas bottom-fermenting yeasts require a temperature of 5-10° C for fermentation, which is only possible in winter without a refrigeration system. The fermentation periods of the two types of yeast also differ greatly. Primary fermentation of top-fermenting yeasts takes two to three days, while bottom-fermenting yeasts require at least a week for fermentation. Because of the longer fermentation time, there is a greater danger that wild yeasts or bacteria will lead to undesirable kinds of fermentation.

> The terms "bottom-fermented" and "top-fermented" are derived from the characteristic nature of each type of yeast. After the brewing process, bottom-fermenting yeasts settle to the bottom of the fermentation vessel, while top-fermenting yeasts create a foam on the surface of the brewing vessel that can be removed.

Yeasts have been developed for the home brewer that combine the qualities of top- and bottom-fermenting yeasts, making it possible, for example, to make bottom-fermented beers at temperatures used by top-fermenting yeasts.

In the breweries the beer yeast is filtered from the finished beer as the yeast remnants can lead to cloudiness and affect the taste. Only recently has there been a trend back to cloudy, unfiltered beers, so-called "*Zwickelbiere*" or "*Hefeweizenbiere*". When brewing at home it is not possible to filter the yeast from the finished beer. The components of the yeast affect the taste

(Photo: www.holzeis.com)

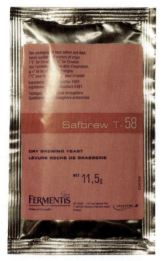

Dry yeast.

and are also very healthy, as beer yeast is the largest provider of vitamins B1, B2, and B6. These water-soluble vitamins of the B-complex have a positive effect on the nerves, skin, and hair. Unfiltered beers also contain more calories (unfortunately) than bland filtered beer.

Today, thousands of different yeast strains are cultivated in special pure yeast facilities, with many breweries procuring yeast strains exclusively for their distinctive beers or breeding yeast in their own laboratories. After each fermentation process the yeast is washed and preserved for subsequent use, a process the breweries call "management" or "yeast management."

> As more yeast fungus is formed during fermentation than was added to the wort before fermentation, one can continue to brew endlessly with the same yeast. As there is a danger of degeneration and faulty fermentation, the yeast is replaced with new pure yeast after five to seven uses.

At home you can certainly use yeast several times if it is kept cool (refrigerator). Certain yeasts can be used several times before optimal fermentation ceases.

Dry Yeast

For home brewing you can purchase dry yeast in packets, similar to the dry yeast used for making bread. Baking yeasts are, after all, relatives of brewing yeasts, which explains why in the Middle Ages beer made by bakers was usually better than elsewhere. There was much more yeast present in the air in bake houses, resulting in a much more controlled fermentation than that of other brewers. A drying process removes the water from dry yeast, therefore it must be dissolved in water before use in order to activate the yeast. The yeast packet contains information as to the activation time and amount of water to be added, as well as for what quantity of beer each packet is sufficient and the optimal fermentation temperature. Dry yeast is certainly the simplest and easiest solution for the home brewer. Always keep a stock of dry yeast in reserve so that you can begin brewing whenever you wish.

As you have no way of knowing how long the dry yeast has been in storage, it is advisable to test the viability of the yeast before using it for fermentation.

TIP

If you are not sure if your dry yeast is viable, test it by adding some to sugar to boiled (sterilized) water that has been cooled to fermentation temperature (0.1 l water and 1 teaspoon of sugar). As yeast turns sugar into alcohol and carbon dioxide, bubbles should appear on the surface within 1 to 2 hours.

Fermentation also gives off a characteristic odor. This test ensures that the yeast is active and will actually turn your wort into beer. Instead of the sugar solution you can also use "Speise" for testing (see page 79).

As mentioned earlier, fermentation produces significantly more yeast than originally added. In breweries this excess yeast is skimmed off and used for subsequent fermentations. Top-fermenting is carefully skimmed from the fermenter; bottom-fermenting yeast settles to the bottom of the fermenter and is taken from there. You can follow the same procedure at home and use the excess yeast from the fermenter, now in the form of liquid yeast, for subsequent fermentations.

Because of the increase in the amount of yeast, you can "harvest" three to four times as much as you originally added to the wort. Theoretically one could continue brewing with this yeast forever. As yeast degenerates, however, at home as in breweries, you should use fresh yeast after several fermentations.

Left: fresh dissolved dry yeast; right: the yeast has settled to the bottom.

Liquid Yeast

This form of yeast is created after the first use of dry yeast and is a brown liquid which smells strongly of beer. Yeast in this form can be added to the wort without further preparation. It should be added at fermentation temperature, therefore top-fermenting yeast should first be brought to room temperature. You can keep the liquid yeast in glass bottles in the refrigerator until needed. Liquid yeast can also be obtained from breweries and small home breweries. There you will receive exact information as to its use and the quantity to be added.

Beer yeast is one of the richest sources for the water-soluble vitamins B1, B2, and B6. You can therefore use the excess yeast as medicine, taking a sip of brewing yeast daily. These vitamins have a positive effect on hair, skin, fingernails, and nerves.

The excess top-fermenting yeast—stored in the refrigerator—can also be used for baking for some time.

Liquid yeast for the home brewer is now commercially available, either in glass tubes ready for use or in plastic packets. The latter contain an activator and are shaken to mix and start the yeast.

The price of these products is somewhat higher than dry yeast. Because of their variety, liquid yeasts are especially well-suited for specialty beers. The taste is also clearly superior to that of dry yeast.

Liquid yeast scooped up from the fermenter.

The Brewing Process in a Brewery

The previous chapter described the raw materials and additives used in the brewing of beer, now we will provide a brief description of the technical process used by breweries to turn these ingredients—water, malt, hops and yeast—into beer.

From the outside, most breweries are typified by large storage buildings, several tall chimneys and—depending on the state of beer production—a strong odor of malt. Most of the big commercial breweries originated from traditional breweries where beer had in some cases been brewed for centuries. Many of these breweries offer tours or even maintain small brewing museums. All of the steps described in this chapter are now carried out with great technological effort, under constant computer-assisted monitoring, observing appropriate hygiene measures, and with corresponding financial expense.

All of these working processes are largely the same for home brewing, even though the size of the necessary equipment cannot be compared with that of the commercial breweries—beginning with the crushing of the malt, through mashing, lautering, boiling, and cooling of the wort, fermentation and bottling of the finished beer, and aging of the young beer in a lagering cellar.

Mashing

Before brewing begins, the mash delivered by the malting house is cleaned, crushed, and mixed with brewing water in the mash pan or fermenter. Most breweries today use the decoction mashing procedure (multiple mash procedure), in which parts of the mash are constantly removed and boiled in the mash pan before being pumped back into the fermenter. At least two mash pans are necessary. The infusion method, on the other hand, only requires one heated mash pan. This process is called "mashing." The malt brew is then heated to 78° C, observing rest periods during which the enzymes in the malt convert the starch into malt sugar. In the brewhouse, the brewmaster constantly observes this saccharification process and uses the iodine test to determine how much malt has formed. An electric agitator ensures that the mash does not stick to the mash vessel and burn.

During mashing the enzymes convert the starch in the malt into malt sugar.

> There are various mashing methods, from simple infusion mashing, in which the temperature is raised to 78° C with appropriate rest periods, to one-, two- and three-mash methods (decoction method), in which parts of the mash are removed, heated separately (boiled) and subsequently added back to the mash.

The infusion method is best suited for home brewing.

The infusion method mentioned at the beginning is best suited for home brewing, as it is the simplest to carry out at home and requires only one mashing pot. The two- and three-mash methods produce a better yield and a better taste variety, which is why commercial breweries use this more costly brewing method.

Many small house and inn breweries also use the simpler infusion method.

Lautering

When the mash has reached its final temperature, the solid elements of the mash (residual grain) are separated from the liquid parts (wort).

> This process is called lautering, whereby the residual grain (the glumes of the barley malt) serves as a natural filter through which the wort flows.

The viscous, slightly sweet wort (pre-wort) is placed in the wort pan, while the grist is washed several times with hot water, the so-called after-wort, in a process referred to as sparging by the brewer. The wort is then thinned with this sparge water (after-wort), which contains many important elements. The remaining grist, which is of no further use in the brewing process, still contains valuable protein components and is valued as high-grade animal feed. Farmers collect this residual grain from the breweries and use it for their feed lot operations.

The Brewing Process (Brewery)

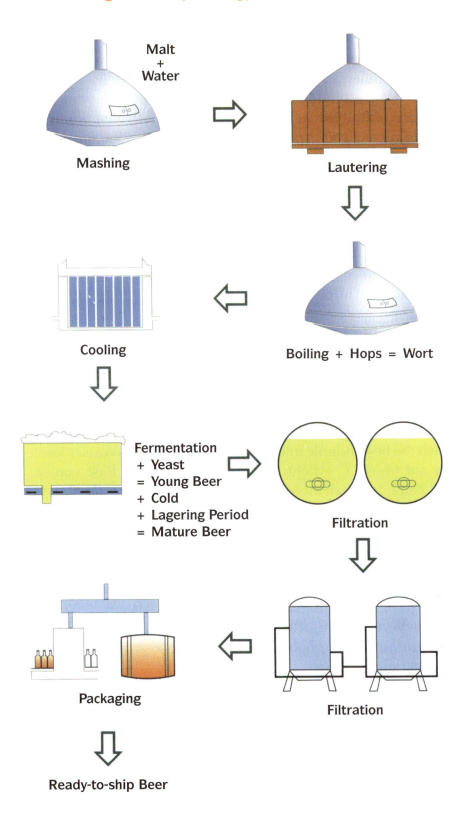

Malt
+
Water

Mashing

Lautering

Boiling + Hops = Wort

Cooling

Fermentation
+ Yeast
= Young Beer
+ Cold
+ Lagering Period
= Mature Beer

Filtration

Filtration

Packaging

Ready-to-ship Beer

*Pumping out the mash
for lautering.*

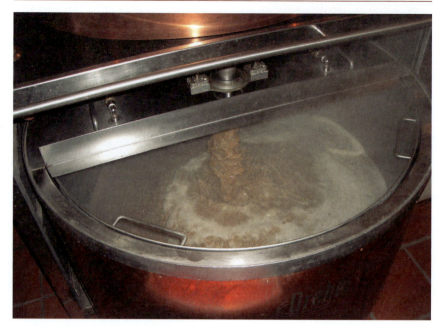

Boiling the Wort

In the wort pan hops are added and the wort is boiled for 1 to 2 hours. In breweries, the wort is boiled in a separate wort or brewing pan in the brewhouse, whereas at home the same pot can be used for mashing and brewing.

As explained in the description of hops, the components of the hops (essential oils) are highly volatile, consequently the brewer does not add all the hops at once, instead adding them in two or three stages.

The hops used depend on the type of beer.

The brewmaster does not add the expensive, high-grade aroma hops until the end of the boiling process, so that as many of their special ingredients as possible are absorbed by the wort. What type or mixture of hops that are used depends on the kind of beer being brewed and are a special art and secrets of the brewmaster.

Boiling releases the flavoring agents in the hops and at boiling temperature the wort is also made sterile. During the boiling process water is lost in the form of steam, which results in re-concentration of the wort (original wort gravity). Thus during boiling the wort gravity, which is the basis for payment of the beer tax, can be determined precisely. However the primary importance of adding hops to the boiling wort is for the removal of protein elements (hot break separation), which is promoted by the hops.

Filtering the Wort

Finally the unwanted proteins are removed from the hot wort in filtering systems or in a whirlpool. The wort is then pumped at high speed horizontally into a large round container. The resulting centrifugal force causes the undissolved elements to form a cone in the center of the whirlpool, from where they can be pumped out. The brewer refers to this as "knocking out."

Cooling and Fermentation of the Beer

The beer is then cooled as quickly as possible to the required fermentation temperature. For bottom-fermented beers the temperature is lowered to 5° C, for top-fermented beers to 20° C. The cooled wort is pumped into fermentation vats (open) or tanks (closed), after which yeast is added and fermentation initiated as quickly as possible. Primary fermentation begins, breaking the malt sugar down into alcohol and carbon dioxide.

> A turbulent process begins after about a day. A thick layer of foam ranging in color from white to yellow forms on the bubbling wort. This foam is called "Kräusen."

The brewmaster regularly checks the state of fermentation using a hydrometer. The more the alcohol concentration in the beer increases, the lower becomes the concentration of the extract (wort extract gravity). Bottom-fermented beers ferment 8-10 days, bottom-fermented beers just 2-3 days, then the primary fermentation is finished. The wort is tested immediately after cooling to determine its specific gravity—which is crucial in determining the beer tax.

Plate filter.

Cool top-fermented beers to 5° C, bottom-fermented beers to 20° C.

Top-fermenting yeast in the fermentation tank of a micro brewery.

Storage of the New Beer and Secondary Fermentation

Fermentation tank.

In the breweries the finished, but still new beer is placed in lagering tanks to mature. In order to guarantee secondary fermentation, so-called "Speise," or unfermented wort, is added to the new beer. Bottom-fermented beers remain in these sealed storage tanks for between three and six months at temperatures close to the freezing point for aging and secondary fermentation.

This "lagering" not only results in the formation of clean beer aromas, it also produces natural carbon dioxide formed by the unfermented wort and the yeast.

The carbon dioxide cannot escape from the sealed lagering tanks. For safety reasons, overpressure valves are installed in the tanks; when pressure inside the tank reaches a predetermined level, the valves allow the excess carbon dioxide to escape.

The finished beer is again filtered, removing the last small impurities and yeast particles. This leaves the beer completely clear and it is subsequently fully-automatically packages in kegs, bottles, cans or containers. Most beers are also pasteurized at 78° C for improved shelf life.

The beer that leaves the brewery is ready to drink and quickly loses quality as a result of lengthy, unsuitable storage at temperatures that are too high and conditions with too much light. Unlike wine, which can be stored for years and whose taste only develops fully after several years, beer is a beverage for immediate or at least early consumption.

Beer quickly loses quality if stored improperly.

Beer is also very sensitive to light and temperature. It is for good reason that dark brown and green bottles have become popular for bottling beer. Beer is best kept in a dark room at 8° C.

Brewing at Home

Whereas the previous pages have given you an idea of how the industrial brewing process works in breweries, in this chapter we will describe how beer is made at home.

The biochemical process that takes place is the same, even though your equipment is very different in terms of size and technical complexity.

Your brewing kettle is a large pot with a capacity of about 20 liters, a cooking spoon (beer paddle) replaces the electric agitator, an industrial filter and/or several cloth diapers, the lauter tun, and the bottling system for you at home is a tube or the outlet valve of a food-safe container. The temperature-control system, usually computer controlled in big breweries, is replaced by a cooking thermometer (digital or analog) at home, and the biochemical monitoring of the brewing process, which in breweries takes place in their own laboratories, can be observed and checked at home using testing reagents from the drugstore by you as "brewmaster."

Before you begin brewing at home, make sure you have all of the necessary utensils and that they work properly. Ensure, if possible, that all bottlenecks are eliminated. Bottlenecks for home brewing include too little time, lack of space, or lack of containers (bottles) for timely bottling of the finished beer. Missing or non-functional equipment can cause all of your efforts to come to nothing.

Many of the steps must be carried out rather quickly, while others demand precise adherence to specified temperatures and rest periods. **Be sure to allow sufficient time for brewing!**

Digital thermometer.
(Photo: www.holzeis.com)

Beer brewing is a process with a division of labor and for many operations, for example the bottling of the finished beer, it is advantageous if someone gives you a hand. Invite a friend to help you brew or brew with your partner. There are always plenty of volunteers to help taste test your beer—why not during brewing as well? You should strive to keep your work spaces and brewing utensils as hygienic as possible. If you intend—as we assume—to brew frequently, we recommend that you use your equipment only for brewing your beer or to procure separate equipment, since bacteria and residue, for example from jams and fruit juices, can lead to faulty fermentation of your beer.

A perusal of the specialty suppliers for the home brewer listed in the pages of appropriate specialist catalogs, or on the internet will quickly give you an idea about necessary and additional useful acquisitions that make brewing much easier and increase enjoyment of your new hobby. Not every article offered for sale is necessary or useful for you initial brewing attempts.

Decide whether you can get by with what you have before investing in expensive equipment.

Before you make expensive purchases, consider how often you intend to brew, what quantities you want to make, and whether you already have the equipment at home needed to make a start. Visiting a gathering on the topic of brewing beer or browsing related pages on the internet can simplify your decision.

Equipment for Home Brewing

The following list will give you a brief overview of the essential equipment for brewing at home. Even in your brewing equipment, the sky is the limit when it comes to your creativity and ingenuity. Brew shops sell so-called beginner's kits, which include a cooking pot, filter material, a food-grade fermentation vat made of plastic with integral spigot, plus a cooking thermometer, a hydrometer, and a fermentation thermometer. Also included are a small bottle of iodine or 1 % potassium iodide solution (iodine colored, not colorless!) for iodine testing, a packet of pH test strips for testing your brewing water and usually also an initial supply of hops, malt and brewing yeast with instructions for your first brewing attempt.

Brewing starter kit.
(Photo: www.holzeis.com)

Cooking Pot

A cooking pot with a capacity of 15-20 liters which can be used equally as well as a mashing pot, a boiler for boiling the wort, and as a fermentation vessel. Particularly suitable are so-called juice-extractors, which are used in the making of fruit juices. These are specially-made items with a capacity of about 20 liters and a thermostat and integral clock. Makers of fruit brandy who have their own boiler, most of which have a capacity of 50 liters or more, can of course use it to prepare the mash and boil the wort. One advantage of electrically-powered boilers is that they permit precise temperature control.

Work space in the hobby room.

Plastic Pail

One or two plastic pails, also with a total capacity of 15-20 liters, used for separating the mash (lautering) and filtering the wort (knock out) after it is boiled. Even better is the use of a food-grade plastic pail, which prevents harmful substances from leeching out of the plastic. The boiling wort has a temperature of about 100° C, which can cause so-called plasticizer (diethyl phthalate) to leach from the plastic of non-food-grade pails. I highly recommend that you procure a fermenting pail, because using its spigot and a tube makes bottling much simpler, it is easier to clean, and saves a considerable amount of time.

Strainer

A strainer, with which the coarse residual grain elements can be filtered out, preventing clogging of the diaper or industrial filter.

Cloth Diapers

Three or four cloth diapers, close-meshed textile fabric or industrial filters for lautering and filtering the wort. Also 20 clothespins for attaching the cloth diapers to the plastic pails.

Cooking Spoon

A large cooking spoon (wood or plastic), or a beer paddle for stirring the mash and the wort.

Refrigerant Gel Packs

Four refrigerant gel packs from coolers or two 1.5-liter plastic soft-drink bottles which are filled with salt water and chilled, in order to cool the wort as quickly as possible to the desired fermentation temperature. For your initial brewing attempts you can also cool the wort in the bathtub, although this method uses much more water.

Beer paddles.
(Photo: www.holzeis.com)

Plastic Tube

A rubber or plastic tube (approx. 1.5 m) for bottling the finished beer. Always clean thoroughly, as bacteria multiply well in the tube resulting in contamination of the beer during bottling. This tube is not necessary when bottling from a fermenting bucket with a spigot, or it can be replaced with a shorter piece of tube about 20 cm long.

Bottles

Sufficient flip-top bottles, kegs or other glass or plastic bottles in which beer can be stored without escape of the carbon dioxide, for storage of the finished beer.

Thermometer

A cooking thermometer which accurately displays the temperature in the 50-100° C range. Also a children's bath thermometer, which is necessary for monitoring the correct fermenting temperature. Temperature range 0-30° C.

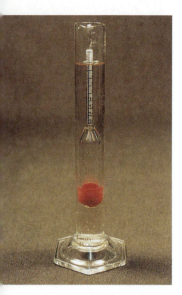

Beer hydrometer.
(Photo: www.holzeis.com)

Iodine Solution

A small bottle of standardized iodine solution for the "iodine test," in order to check the saccharification of the malt, or 1 % potassium iodide solution (iodine-colored, not colorless!). These chemical reagents are available at any pharmacy or from brew shops. Pharmacies also carry Betaisadona solution for disinfecting wounds, which can also be used for the iodine test.

pH Test Strips

A packet of pH test paper for checking the pH value of the brewing water. You can also inquire about the pH level of your water at the local waterworks.

Beer Hydrometer

A beer hydrometer for measuring the specific gravity of the wort and the determining when the beer is ready to be bottled. There are hydrometers with integral temperature indicators, which can make the children's bath thermometer unnecessary. Beer hydrometers are usually calibrated to a temperature of 20° C (for top-fermented beers).

Lauter tun for home brewing.
(Photo: www.holzeis.com)

Other Useful Equipment

After your first tries at brewing you will discover that the above-described equipment—which is no more than basic equipment—has its weaknesses when brewing larger quantities of beer. Lautering is one of the biggest problems when brewing at home, however this can be overcome with some effort. The cloth diapers can be replaced with industrial filters or gauze mesh with a diameter of 1 mm, which result in better separation of sediment from the wort.

Lautering Tun

A dedicated lautering tun with integral spigot greatly simplifies the task of separating the mash and the wort.

Cooking pot, thermometer, cooking spoon, iodine, cloth diapers, pH test strips.

Fermenting Pail

A large fermenting pail, which can also be used as a lautering tun, with a spigot greatly simplifies the bottling process. Ensure that the fermenting pail is made of food-grade plastic, otherwise harmful substances (plasticizer and solvents) can leach from the plastic during alcoholic fermentation.

Cooled Fermentation Chamber

It is recommended that you convert a refrigerator or old freezer into a cooled fermentation chamber for bottom-fermented beers, for only with electric refrigeration is it possible to make bottom-fermented beers all year long.

Small Brewing Systems for the Home and Pub Brewer

Recent years have seen the development of semi-professional brewing systems for home brewers and micro-breweries, which in terms of price are definitely an alternative to cooking pots, fermenting pails, and do-it-yourself work. Well thought-out, space-saving solutions make possible electronically-monitored brewing processes and much more precise and reproducible brewing results. Some of these small brewing systems are even used by major breweries for trying out small quantities of new recipes, a process much too expensive in the large industrial systems. For years now there have also been beer brewing championships in the German-speaking countries for home and micro-breweries, most of which use these small brewing systems (see page 105).

> Before you begin brewing—and of course during every subsequent brewing process—ensure that all of your equipment and tools are on hand and fully functional!

Fermenter with air lock. (Photo: www.holzeis.com)

Modern home-brewing system. (Photo: www.holzeis.com)

Work Spaces

In breweries different temperatures are maintained in the brew house and the lagering cellar.

In most cases, the kitchen is used for brewing at home. Before starting, it should always be borne in mind that the kitchen, and the stove in particular, will be occupied for at least 4 to 5 hours. In a brewery the various steps are intentionally separated, as different conditions and temperatures prevail in the brewhouse and fermenting cellar during filtering of the beer and bottling. You should keep this in mind when brewing at home and seek out appropriate spaces in the house. A separate work or hobby room with its own power, water, and drain connections is certainly the best solution. There you can brew undisturbed and without bothersome time constraints, and without having to worry about limitations as in the kitchen.

Obviously you make do with the space available to you, whereby one may have to lower one's sights from the optimum.

We do not wish to suggest that brewing beer at home does not create a certain amount of mess. Crushing and mashing the malt produces a some dust, whereas mashing the malt produces malt sugar, which, as we know, is very sticky in liquid form. During lautering and filtering of the wort, it is almost impossible to avoid spilling a few drops of the sweet, sticky liquid onto your equipment, especially the stove. Use caution with glass cooktops on electric stoves; if the sugary solution burns onto the ceramic plates, the residue is difficult to remove. A separate hotplate or a camping stove are better suited and easier to clean than the kitchen stove.

Brewing at home makes a certain amount of mess.

In the summer you can brew in the backyard or on the balcony, surely an attraction for a pleasant barbecue with friends. This has the advantage of avoiding a mess in the house. Small cellar rooms are best for fermentation; less well suited are garages and parking areas. As beer readily absorbs foreign smells, use of the latter may result in gasoline and paint fumes imparting unwanted tastes to your beer.

Fermentation Room, Fermentation Cellar

Room temperatures of 20° C are desirable for fermenting top-fermented beers.

The area used for fermentation must meet certain requirements. Even though electric cooling is not needed for brewing top-fermented beer, a room temperature of about 60° F/15° C is desirable. A room in the basement surely meets these requirements better than the kitchen, where the temperature is usually over 70° F/20° C. You can regulate the temperature with refrigerant gel packs or frozen plastic bottles, but a cool room in the basement with the appropriate ambient temperature is certainly better.

Boiling Heat Source

To boil your mash and later the wort at the necessary temperature you need a heat source that delivers sufficient energy in a reasonable time in order to achieve and maintain the required temperatures. Whether you use a gas or electric stove is secondary.

Performance of the device must be sufficient to bring the wort to a boil. The minimum requirement is 1,000 to 1,500 Watts. Energy delivery should be such that a rate of temperature increase of 1° C per minute can be achieved during mashing.

Cooking pot with thermostat. (Photo: www.holzeis.com)

Both stoves have advantages and disadvantages. The gas stove has a decisive advantage in that temperature is easier to control, as the desired temperature can be maintained more precisely by increasing or lowering the flame. With an electric stove, when the temperature is set the burners usually retain residual heat, which usually results in temperature rising above the desired rest temperature during rest periods. Shutting the burner off before the desired temperature is reached allows better use to be made of this residual heat, and the cooking pot does not always have to be removed from the stove before the desired temperature is achieved.

Also remember that—due to physical reasons—the mash on the surface of the mash pot is warmer than in the middle of the liquid. Thermometers that only measure the temperature in the upper region can therefore show clear temperature deviations.

Digital thermometers measure the temperature in the middle of the liquid and are even equipped with acoustic temperature indicators which sound when the target temperature is reached.

An electric juicer with integral thermostat, which is heated electrically through a double base, is a particularly suitable boiling medium. There are juicers with an integral clock, so that the desired rest period and temperature can be predetermined and precisely set. A semi-automatic home brewery! An excellent combination is the use of fruit brandy boilers for mashing and boiling the wort. The temperature can be precisely controlled and they usually have sufficient capacity for brewing beer. Another advantage is that the brandy stills are not used year round, resulting in better exploitation of this technical system.

If you use your own work or hobby room for your brewing efforts, you should—so that you do not need to use an old stove—use a gas camp stove or electric hotplate with the necessary performance level. If the small cooker's performance is not sufficient to bring the wort to a rolling boil, you can also employ an electric immersion heater which is suspended in the wort. Normally, however, the performance of these electric hotplates and gas cookers is sufficient to bring 20 liters of wort to a boil in a reasonable time.

Small "home brewery." (Photo: www.holzeis.com)

To save energy and reach boiling temperature more easily and faster, you should always place a cover on your mash and wort pot (until the addition of hops). During the mashing process, however, you must constantly stir the mash to prevent it burning to the bottom of the mash pot.

Here, too, there are suggestions from do-it-yourselfers, who have designed and installed agitators in their mash pots and thus automated the boring and time-consuming task of stirring the mash. Painters use similar devices to stir their paint.

Remove the pot lid when boiling the wort so that excess hop oils can escape.

Therefore you will have to repeatedly remove the cover; on the other hand, when boiling the wort, after boiling temperature had been reached and the hops added the pot lid is removed so that excess hop oils can escape the boiling wort. Otherwise these would make the flavor of the beer too bitter. This also reduces the danger of the wort boiling over.

Especially remember to place your pot as flat as possible on the burner to ensure the best possible transfer of energy from the burner to the pot.

Hygiene

A very important point in beer brewing is cleanliness and the associated care of brewing equipment. Beer is made by using living substances (yeast), which react extremely sensitively to less than optimal brewing conditions. Hygiene-related contaminants such as mold, bacteria—especially lactic acid bacteria, the bane of brewers for centuries—and dirt not only compromise taste and aroma, but also lead to faulty fermentation, which can render your beer totally undrinkable. All of your labor and outlay can therefore be brought to nothing by inadequate hygiene, as your beer can be spoiled and there are no technical aids to make it drinkable again. Spoiled beer can only be disposed of.

Take care to ensure that conditions in your brewing and fermenting rooms, in particular, are hygienic.

Hand cleaning bottles with a bottle brush.

As mentioned quite a few times, there are sufficient "wild yeasts" in normal air to initiate spontaneous fermentation. Once they gain a foothold, such yeasts gain the upper hand and suppress the desired work of the pure yeast added to your wort. On the other hand, this spontaneous fermentation is intentionally brought about in making certain specialty beers (Belgian lambic and geuze beers), but this requires a great deal of skill and experience on the part of the brewer. *Berliner Weiße* is also made using a mixture of yeast and lactic acid, usually undesired and feared by brewers.

All equipment that comes into direct contact with the beer, such as pots, pails, cooking spoons, thermometers, colanders and filters, or the beer hydrometer, must be carefully cleaned and kept as free as possible of germs and bacteria. After each brewing session, therefore, thoroughly clean your mashing and wort pot with hot water. Then thoroughly rinse with cold water and wash again with hot water before use.

In breweries special cleaners are used to clean the brewing equipment, the brewing kettle, the lines, vats and fermenting tanks, and after these cleaning steps everything is thoroughly rinsed with hot and then cold water in order to remove any residue from equipment and lines.

> Fat-containing household cleaners (dishwashing detergent) are not recommended for care of brewing equipment, as the fatty residue sticks to the utensils and can leach into the mash and wort during the brewing process.

Boiling rubber seals.

These fat-containing detergents destroy the water's surface tension and this can prevent home-brewed beer from forming a proper head when poured. The same applies to bottles and beer glasses, which should also not be cleaned with these detergents or in dishwashers. The catering industry uses special cleaning agents, and you have surely noticed that in good restaurants the server carefully rinses the empty glass with cold water before pouring the beer to remove any possible detergent residue. Vinegar-based cleaning agents are also unsuitable for cleaning brewing equipment, as there is the danger that vinegar bacteria can make the beer sour. The use of washing soda for cleaning brewing equipment at home is safe and effective. This naturally-occurring cleaning agent is also extremely cost-effective.

Before pouring a beer, the landlord rinses the glass to remove possible detergent residue.

> Various cleaning and sterilizing agents are available from restaurant supply stores and home brewing shops. These can be used to create optimal hygienic conditions for brewing at home.

In most cases, however, cleaning your equipment thoroughly with hot water and possibly some soda solution, then rinsing with clear, cold water before each brewing process is sufficient.

Crushing the Malt

In the previous chapter on the brewing process in breweries, you were given a brief overview of the malting process, which is now carried out in most breweries by service providers—their own malthouses. For brewing at home you do not require the same huge quantities as commercial or industrial breweries, which procure their malt by the truckload from the malthouses. In an internet search of home brewing resources, you will find suppliers of malt, hops, and yeast which specialize in the needs of the burgeoning market for the home brewer.

These middlemen buy large quantities of malt, process (crush) it and package it in manageable quantities. They also offer different malt mixtures for a wide variety of beers and usually also offer all of the technical equipment such as beer hydrometers, thermometers, bottles, cleaners and specialist literature.

Of course this work has its price, and purchasing small quantities and the not inconsiderable delivery costs can make your home-brewed beer quite expensive.

If there is a small microbrewery in your area, or even a commercial brewery, we recommend that you get in touch with the brewmaster or proprietor there and ask him for malt, hops, and yeast for your brewing efforts. Based on our information, most of these small microbreweries are quite happy to sell you the necessary quantities of malt, and often the local brewmaster, himself a professional, can offer you useful tips. The breweries have by now realized that the small home brewer, with a capacity of about 20 liters, is no competition for the local breweries. On the contrary, the more you know about making beer and brewing secrets, the better you

Grain mills are suitable for crushing malt.

will be able to appreciate a well-made and served beer. Procuring raw materials from these sources is much more economical, as there are no transport or processing fees. You can also be sure that the brewing malt is freshly crushed and has not suffered from lengthy transport times and improper storage.

As we have discovered, large malthouses are also willing to deliver brewing malt to retail customers or sell it to them directly. As the minimum quantity is a 50-kg bag, it is perhaps better to purchase the malt together with one or more other home brewers.

Malt mill for home breweries.
(Photo: www.holzeis.com)

Uncrushed malt, as offered by the malthouses, keeps for some time, whereas crushed malt has a limited shelf life as the enzymes in the malt become inactive after a certain time and can no longer, or only insufficiently, break down the starch into malt sugar.

A disadvantage of buying uncrushed malt, however, is that it must be processed (crushed) before brewing can begin, which can cause considerable difficulties at home. Breweries have their own malt-mills, which can grind the malt to any desired size. If you have a grain mill used for milling grain for the making of bread or for preparing cereal, you can also use it to crush your brewing malt by setting the mill on its coarsest setting. With it you can easily crush enough malt for 10-20 liters of beer. Some kitchen food processors come with an attachment for turning grain into flakes. You can use this to crush your brewing malt, although the process creates a significant quantity of dust as such devices do not usually operate in enclosed systems. Hand-operated coffee grinders are somewhat suitable for crushing, however the effort needed to crush 3 to 5 kg of malt is not inconsiderable. Completely unsuitable, on the other hand, are electric coffee grinders, as the crushing cannot be precisely controlled and moreover the performance of the machine is hopelessly overtaxed by the quantity to be processed. With certain limitations, kitchen tools such as graters for processing nuts and crushers for making grain flakes can also be used for crushing the malt.

Brew shops now offer a number of malt-mills for the home brewer, an investment that will only pay off after a number of brewing sessions. Of course freshly-crushed malt is better than malt that has been crushed for some time.

As described in the chapter on crushing in a brewery, it is possible to minimize the amount of dust created by soaking the malt in water overnight or at least for several hours. The water should not be warmer than 8-10° C, however, so as not to activate the enzymes prematurely. Malt ground in this way cannot be stored and must be used immediately.

The simplest solution for the home brewer, therefore, is to buy malt that has been crushed and sealed in airtight packaging.

After it has been soaked in water, the malt can be crushed without the formation of an excessive amount of dust.

Mashing the Malt

Having discussed the purely technical requirements for home brewing, such as work spaces, hygiene, and brewing utensils, we will now begin describing the actual process of brewing.

The first step—as in the breweries—is the mashing or mashing in of the malt, in which the crushed malt is mixed with prepared brewing water (the hardness and pH value of the water must be correct).

The temperature—depending on the brewing method being used—is raised to the mashing temperature of 35-50° C while stirring constantly with the cooking spoon.

1-3: mashing;
4: checking mash
temperature.

The constant movement, produced by an electric agitator in a brewery, is necessary in order to prevent the malt from settling to the bottom of the pot and burning. This mechanical movement also helps the elements important to brewing to better dissolve in the brewing water.

The quantities of water for mashing given in the recipes are only approximate figures. The mash must not be too thick, so as to prevent it from settling in the brew pot, while at the same time it must not be too thin as heating a larger quantity of mash will consume significantly more energy.

Infusion Method

In the brewing diagram (page 111), you will once again see—depicted graphically—the rest times at various temperatures, here for example for the infusion method. This method is best suited for brewing at home, as just one mash pot is required. The temperature is steadily raised while adhering to the prescribed rest times.

Once a particular mash temperature is reached, there follows a rest period of about 15 minutes, the so-called protein rest. During this rest the crushed brewing malt swells in the brewing water and the enzymes in the malt are activated by the brewing water and the heat.

A pleasant aroma—similar to that of Ovaltine—begins to fill the brewing space. It is difficult to imagine that this pale, light-brown brew, which smells like the children's drink, will eventually become a bitter, clear beer.

After the protein rest the temperature of the mash is raised to 64° C—again while stirring constantly.

The formation of maltose (malt sugar) begins at this temperature, therefore the subsequent rest period of about half an hour is also called the first saccharification or starch conversion rest. Maltose is the fermentable sugar which determines the strength of the beer. The longer the saccharification rest, the more malt sugar forms, resulting in stronger beer. In addition to using an iodine test, you can taste-test the liquid to check the formation of maltose. As the mashing process proceeds, you will find—assuming the enzymes in the brewing malt are working properly—the mash liquid becoming ever sweeter. The iodine test is more precise and in any case more reliable.

> By taste-testing you can determine that the mash is still sweet.

The iodine test is essentially a chemical experiment to determine if maltose and dextrin are being formed by the enzymes in the brewing malt.

The technical term for this is "protein breakdown." The iodine test, which should be carried out during the first and second saccharification rest, will be described in greater detail at the conclusion of the mashing procedure. The iodine test should be carried out no matter which brewing method—infusion or decoction—is used and the results entered in your brewing log.

> The iodine test should be carried out during the first and second saccharification rests.

After the first saccharification rest, the temperature of the mash is raised to 72° C. This is followed by another break, the second saccharification rest, which, again, lasts about half an hour.

During this second saccharification rest dextrin, the second form of sugar, is formed by the enzymes in the brewing malt along with maltose. Dextrin is a non-fermentable sugar and gives the beer its richness. The longer the second saccharification rest, the more full-bodied (possibly also sweeter) the finished beer will be.

After this second saccharification rest, the temperature is raised again, to 78° C, followed by another half-hour rest period, after which the first step in home brewing, mashing, is completed.

Decoction Method

In contrast to the previously described infusion method, in which the temperature of the mash is increased by constant warming, in the decoction method parts of the mash are removed from the mash pot after mashing and brought to a boil in a separate pot.

As a rule of thumb, about one-third of the mash is removed and brought to a boil.

The mash is boiled more fiercely in the decoction method than in the infusion method.

In this boiling process the malt in the mash is boiled more fiercely than in the infusion method, consequently the yield of finished beer is somewhat greater for the same quantity of malt than with the significantly simpler infusion method.

The minimum technical requirement for employing the decoction method at home is a second pot in which to boil part of the mash. The requirement to transfer mash from one pot to another increases the likelihood of making a mess in your work space. The sweet, sticky liquid splashes readily when being poured from the cooking pot. In breweries, which employ a closed system, the boiling mash is pumped back into the mash pan.

When using this mashing method ensure that when the boiling mash is returned the temperature of the combined mash does not exceed 72° C, otherwise the enzymes in the brewing malt will be killed prematurely.

This process of removing some of the mash and boiling it separately is continued until the mash mixture temperature reaches 78° C. Then—as in the infusion method—there follows a rest period of about half an hour before the mash is lautered.

The mash should be allowed to rest for half an hour before lautering.

You will have to decide for yourself which of these brewing methods you use at home. On the one hand, this mashing method produces a somewhat greater yield and allows a wider variety of flavors to be achieved than the infusion method, while, on the other, it requires a certain amount of experience to be able to estimate the correct quantity of mash for removal and the temperature when it is returned. As well, somewhat more energy is required to raise the temperature of the mash to 78° C at home, as energy is lost if the mash pot is not appropriately insulated, and to bring the separated part of the mash to a boil.

We recommend the simpler infusion method for your first brewing efforts. You can experiment with the decoction method if you already have some brewing experience.

Iodine Test

The iodine test confirms the breakdown of starch in the brewing malt.

The iodine test is used to determine to what degree sugars, namely maltose and dextrin, have formed from the brewing malt. These two types of sugar are needed so that they can be broken down into carbon dioxide and alcohol during fermentation. In proper chemical terms, one is not checking the formation of sugar, rather the breakdown of starch in the brewing malt, followed in turn by the formation of the two simple sugars maltose and dextrin. If the mash contains too much starch, the iodine solution will turn purple to dark blue, whereas too little starch will result in a yellow color (straw-yellow).

Despite its very technical and complicated-sounding name, carrying out the iodine test is quite simple.

> During the first saccharification rest at 64° C remove several drops of liquid and place them on a white plate or saucer. One drop of iodine solution (1 % potassium iodide, iodine-colored, not clear!) is dropped into this liquid, after which the small plate is shaken to combine them.

Standardized iodine solution, which is used to disinfect wounds under the name Betaisadona Solution and is inexpensive and available in any pharmacy, is also ideally suited for carrying out the iodine test. The resulting color of the liquid allows you to determine the level of starch conversion. The iodine test—which takes only a few minutes—should be carried out more once, at a variety of temperatures, in order to be able to confirm the starch conversion process. It should be checked at least once more after the second saccharification rest at 72° C. Even better, however, are tests at 64° C after the first saccharification rest and at 78° C at the *end of the mashing process*.

Standard iodine solution is best suited for performing the iodine test.

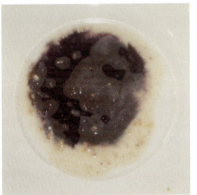 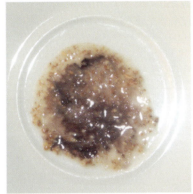 

If the test result is still blue and the mash has only a slight sweet taste, conversion of the malt into malt sugar by the enzymes has not taken place, or at least *not to a sufficient extent*.

No saccharification has taken place (left) Start of saccharification (center). Yellow color means that malt sugar has formed from the malt.

> If no malt sugar has formed, the brewing yeast will not be able to produce alcohol and carbon dioxide.

In most cases the mash test will result in a yellow color after some time. If this does not happen, it is either because of the malt and, in turn, poor enzymes (storing the crushed malt for too long destroys the enzymes), or you failed to adhere exactly to the mashing temperatures and prescribed rests and the enzymes were unable to break down the starch in the brewing malt. In both cases, which happen only rarely, the mash is unsuitable for making beer and can no longer be used.

If the rest periods are not adhered to precisely, the enzymes cannot break down the starch.

You can see how important this minor excursion into chemistry, the iodine test, is during the mashing of the brewing malt in ensuring that the brew actually becomes beer. Once again we would like to remind you to make notes in your brewing log, in which the results of the iodine test at each temperature should be recorded. This is the only way to identify possible brewing and fermentation errors and prevent them in them future. If the iodine test is positive, you can be sure that no errors have been made as maltose and dextrin have formed.

Lautering the Mash

As in breweries, the mashing procedure is followed by lautering of the mash.

Pre-straining using a colander.

"Lautering" is understood as separation of the solid elements (grist) from the liquid elements (wort) of the mash.

In breweries, this lautering process is a very time-consuming procedure in which the mash is pumped into a separate lauter tun whose bottom has small holes or slots through which the liquid wort can flow. It is then mixed with hops in the wort pan and boiled. This process takes three to four hours, during which the solid elements of the residual grain (brewing malt hulls) are used as a natural filter through which the wort must flow. Barley malt in particular is very well suited as a natural filter, which is why mixtures containing barley malt are used in other beers.

Cloth diapers, which are stretched over a bucket and used as a filtering material, will suffice for your first brewing efforts. Use clothespins to attach the diaper to the rim of the bucket. Use your hand to create a depression about 10 cm deep in the middle of the diaper, so that you can see when the pail is full.

Lautering through a diaper.

The process is much easier if you use a simple colander to roughly separate the wort from the grist before filtering through the cloth diaper.

Lautering using an industrial filter (fine mesh).

The colander has the advantage of trapping the coarser elements of the mash, preventing them from immediately clogging the cloth diaper. The residue in the diaper is removed by simultaneously removing the clothespins and lifting all four corners of the diaper. Depending on the amount of mash, you may need several containers for interim storage of the wort. Carefully twist the diaper and squeeze the mash residue in the diaper. The "diaper method" will provide satisfactory results for batches of 10 to 20 liters. If you intend to brew more frequently or make larger batches of beer, however, you will soon reach the limits of the diaper's capacity. As an alternative, suppliers of home brewing equipment offer plastic industrial filters that are sewn together like funnels or bags. These make it relatively easy to separate

Separating the wort from the mash using a lauter tun.

the wort, which has been pre-strained through a colander. These cone- or bag-shaped filters are easy to empty and clean with water, making possible a better and above all faster process than with cloth diapers.

Transferring the hot mash from the mash pot by means of a smaller container holding between a half liter and a liter instead of pouring it directly into the filter will also make the job easier.

ATTENTION!	Burn risk!

After the heavier elements of the mash—the grist—have sunk to the bottom of the mash pot, the liquid components of the wort can be removed relatively easily. The remaining residue is returned to the empty mash pot and hot water is added. This process, called sparging, helps remove remaining useful elements of the mash (mainly maltose). The sparge water (in the quantity specified in the recipe or required to produce the desired amount of beer) should also be heated to 78° C. Use your cooking spoon to stir the grist well in order to release as many important brewing components from the grist as possible.

Removing the mash for lautering using a small measuring container.

Breaking up the residual grain in the colander or lauter tun.

Sparging with hot water.

A self-designed lauter tun with metal strainer and spigot.

After lautering clean the mash pot with hot water in preparation for returning the wort.

Another way of separating the solid and liquid components of the mash is to stretch a cloth or a diaper over an overturned table, attached to the table legs, with a container placed beneath this "filter." This method lautering has the decisive advantage of enabling you to watch the container and see when it is full and needs to be emptied. Also, an overturned table is more stable than a bucket as it has a larger resting surface and therefore less danger of tipping over.

Lauter Tun

If you intend to make beer from time to time, the above-described "diaper method" has several disadvantages. The separation is pure manual labor and very time consuming, and lautering by means of a diaper allows relatively many impurities into the wort, which can cause problems during fermentation and negatively affect the taste of the beer.

By making your own lauter tun it is possible to automate, or at least partly automate, the time-intensive lautering process.

A lauter tun should have a spigot at the bottom through which the filtered wort can flow. On the bottom of the lauter tun there is an exact-fitting insert with many small holes or slots with a maximum diameter of 1 to 1.5 mm. The solid elements of the residual grain sink to the bottom and act as a natural filter, through which the wort is clarified and can seep. Of course your inventiveness and craft skills have free rein in improving and constructing such lautering devices. In designing such equipment, always ensure that the holes in the insert are large enough to allow the wort to drain in a reasonable time, but small enough to hold back the solid residue from the mash.

The solid elements of the residual grain form a natural filter.

If you have a juicer for making fruit juices, you can easily convert it into a simple lauter tun. Such juicers already have an insert with holes and a drain cock with plastic tube. An industrial filter or a gauze mesh with 1-millimeter diameter holes can be placed over the insert, whose holes are too large.

Plastic food-grade cider jars for apple juice have an insert which floats on the liquid to delay fermentation of the juice. You can simply use a drill to put 1-mm diameter holes in the insert, resulting in a cheap lauter tun capable of separating the liquid from the grist, as an integral spigot enables controlled lautering.

If all of this seems like too much work, brewing shops can provide an alternative. Lauter tuns made of plastic, but also of stainless steel, can be purchased at affordable prices.

Using a fruit juicer as a lauter tun.

Boiling the Wort

After lautering the mash you have liquid wort, which is used in the third step, boiling the wort.

The wort consists of the first wort, which is filtered directly from the grist, and the second wort.

Pour the wort into the clean cooking pot.

The solid elements of the mash—the residual grain—were washed out with the sparge water and now have no more use in brewing your beer. This grist still contains a number of important components, which can be used in feeding humans or animals. Large breweries have contracts with feed lots or farmers, who use this byproduct of beer making as a feed additive for their animals. In the Middle Ages the grist was mixed with flour and used to make so-called "*Treberbrot*" (spent grain bread). A few small craft breweries that still mainly use the infusion method of brewing (in which the grist is not so heavily boiled) today offer *Treberbrot* as a special delicacy with their beer. The grist (30-40%) is mixed with sour dough (or baking yeast) and is baked as bread or cakes. In fresh condition—before the grist begins to ferment—it is added to muesli, providing valuable fiber for human consumption.

The waste from your home brewing can of course be fed to chickens, cows, or pigs, or you can compost it as bio-waste. As beer is made with all-natural ingredients, your small-scale home brewing causes no harm to the environment through waste or chemical substances.

The wort at a rolling boil.

The elements of the hops important for brewing dissolve into the wort.

Adding the hops.

Hop pellets and liquid hops are more economical than natural hops.

The wort is now emptied back into the clean cooking pot (mash pot) and brought to a boil as quickly as possible.

> To save energy, you should cover the cooking pot with a suitable cover until the addition of the hops. This prevents too much water from evaporating during the boil and allows a rolling boil for the hops.

Boiling the wort inevitably results in the loss of some water in the form of steam, however, the important extracts of the beer such as maltose, dextrin, and the added hop components remain in the wort. This results in a higher concentration of these extract components (specific gravity), and the specific gravity of the wort can be adjusted by adding water of the specific boiling away of water. By removing a small amount of wort and cooling it to 20° C (beer hydrometers are usually calibrated to this temperature) you can use your hydrometer to accurately measure the specific gravity and, if necessary, adjust it to the desired gravity of your beer; upwards—by boiling away water—or downwards—by adding water. A detailed description of how to use the beer hydrometer begins on page 82.

When the wort begins to boil, the specified variety and quantity of hops is added to the boiling wort.

> Experienced brewers do not add all the hops at once, instead dividing them into two or three parts, with the highest quality and thus most expensive hop varieties not being added to the wort until the end of the boil (1 – 1 ½) hours.

As previously described in the chapter on raw materials on page 25 ff., hops can be purchased in various forms (pellets, hop powder, tried natural hops or liquid hops) which differ greatly from one another in terms of quality, flavor and especially intensity.

Use caution in dosage of hops in order to avoid unpleasant taste surprises with respect to sourness or bitterness.

RULE OF THUMB:

The more hops, the more bitter the finished beer.

Hop pellets, which are hop powder in concentrated form, and liquid hops are more economical than dried natural hops, for example. In most cases, the type designation and the information packaged with your hops will reveal the quality and especially the intensity of this delicate agricultural product. The recipes in this book include the BE or IBU values as rough reference points for the various beer varieties.

During the entire boiling process, growing amounts of hops adhere to the sides of the pot and these should carefully be stirred back into the wort from time to time using the cooking spoon. Take care to maintain a light rolling boil, but not so much that the sticky-sweet wort boils over.

Boiling of the wort serves, on the one hand, to sterilize it, as boiling at about 100° C for one to one-and-a-half hours kills germs and bacteria, while, on the other hand, boiling also releases the characteristic bitter substances of the hops, transferring their distinctive flavoring notes to the wort and ultimately the finished beer. The essential oils of the hop are extremely volatile and very many of these ingredients are lost during the boil. In the end only about 20% of the bitter substances from the hops remain in the finished beer. This explains why the most expensive aroma hops are not added until the end of the wort boiling process, to ensure that their high-grade flavoring components make their way into the finished beer.

> Boiling the wort also causes the precipitation of protein elements, which are filtered from the wort during the subsequent filtering and cooling (hot break removal).

While the wort is boiling, you can make preparations for the next step in the brewing process, carefully cleaning the bucket and filter, stretching fresh clean diapers over the bucket and checking possible cooling equipment, such as ice-water bottles and refrigerant gel packs.

Boiling the wort serves to sterilize the solution and release the bittering substances in the hops.

Speise (Unfermented Wort) for Secondary Fermentation

If you intend to work with speise, you must now prepare several bottles for filling with the hot wort. As the exact timing for bottling beer does not always fall into every home brewer's schedule, the use of speise for secondary fermentation in bottles, kegs, and cans is an interesting alternative. Bottling beer at one in the morning or just before sunrise is not to everyone's taste.

Speise can be used to bring about secondary fermentation in the bottled beer.

> Speise is taken from the still-hot wort (caution: risk of burning!) and placed in the cleaned swing-top bottles.

Use no more than 5-10% of the brew, or 1–2 liters of hot wort from a 20-liter batch, and place it in clean bottles; a correspondingly smaller amount from smaller batches. Use a towel or oven mitts to protect your hands while handling the hot wort. Seal the bottles immediately. Invert the bottles to allow the hot wort to sterilize the bottle opening and then store in a cool place.

The speise is added to the new beer immediately after the end of primary fermentation, just before the containers are filled.

Approximately 5-10% of the wort is used for the speise.

The speise provides sufficient nourishment for the yeast still in the new beer (Speise = food, hence the name) to produce sufficient pressure inside the bottle. As the CO_2 cannot escape from the sealed bottle, secondary fermentation produces refreshing carbon dioxide.

The beer should still contain sufficient fermentable substances after bottling.

There is a window of opportunity of just a few hours for bottling the new beer, during which sufficient fermentable substances remain in the beer to result in enrichment and secondary fermentation. With the speise method you have a buffer and can bottle the new beer at your leisure after the end of primary fermentation.

You are advised to attend a beer brewing course or workshop for hobby brewers, as these old hobby brewing methods and tricks are often discussed there.

Filtering and Cooling the Wort

After filtering, cool the wort to the desired fermentation temperature.

After the boiling of the wort, the next step in the home brewing process is filtering and then cooling the wort to the desired fermenting temperature. As described in detail in the chapter titled "Lautering," filtering is done through fresh, clean cloth diapers, which are stretched over pails and fixed in place with clothespins. Filtering the hot wort removes hop residue and protein (hot break) from the wort.

Filtering makes the wort relatively clear, and the finer the filtering is, the better will be the fermentation of the cooled wort by the yeast.

Protein remnants, mash residue and hop elements hamper or prevent proper alcoholic fermentation.

Filtering the wort (left); Hop residue (center); Protein, mash and hop residue (right)

> **CAUTION!**
>
> Take care to avoid scalding yourself when removing the hot wort from the cooking pot.

It is now important to cool the filtered wort as quickly as possible to the fermenting temperature to prevent wild yeasts or bacteria, which are in the air, from reproducing in the wort. There are several different ways of cooling the wort. Emptying the buckets back into the clean pot and then back into the buckets several times will lower the temperature of the wort to about 60° C. Below this temperature the procedure becomes ineffective. You can now place the pot with the warm wort in the bathtub and cool it from the outside with cold running water, or place it in a plastic tub containing cold water and cool it with cold running water, whereby the cooling water runs over the rim of the tub and down the drain. Emptying should take place outside, as the temperature reduction will usually take place more quickly there and the danger of making a mess is reduced.

Wort chillers made of copper or steel tubing, which are connected to the water line and submerged in the hot wort, cool the wort using the counterflow principle. The warm water that flows out the other end of the coil can be used to clean your equipment. A coiled plastic, or even better rubber, tube through which liquid can flow achieves similar cooling results, although copper tubing transfers heat more efficiently.

Wort chiller
(Photo: www.holzeis.com)

> Pay particular attention to hygiene at this stage, as the wort is now especially vulnerable to bacteria and wild yeasts.

Another relatively simple method of quickly cooling the hot wort is to place refrigerant gel packs or large plastic soda bottles (1.5–2 liters), which are made of food-grade plastic and can be filled with water and frozen in the freezer, directly into the wort. This method is ideally suited for cooling the wort to 15-20° C for top fermenting yeasts, as the fermentation process releases energy in the form of heat which in turn raises the fermenting temperature. For hygienic reasons the bottles and refrigerant gel packs should be rinsed with hot water to prevent transferring bacteria from them to the hot wort.

Cooling the wort causes a few more solid elements to separate, which can be filtered out by refiltering through a clean cloth diaper.

Cooling the boiled wort in cold running water.

Measuring Specific Gravity

You have surely seen information on "specific gravity" in percent and alcohol content in percentage by volume on the labels of beer bottles. While the two values are indirectly connected they are not to be confused.

> An specific gravity of 12% or degrees—a typical lager beer—means, for example, that 1 liter (1000 grams) of wort contains 120 g of dissolved matter (extracts) and 880 grams of water.

Determining the degree of fermentation. Hydrometer (left). A coffee filter is used to filter out carbon dioxide – carbon dioxide affects the buoyancy of the hydrometer and results in an inaccurate hydrometer reading (right).

According to the German Beer Tax Law as well as the Austrian and Swiss laws, this specific gravity is the basis for calculating the quantity- and strength-based beer tax. For the exact laws concerning brewing at home, see page 146. These laws contain a minimum wort content for each category of beer, which cannot be fallen short of under any circumstances. These rules don't mean much to the home brewer as his beer is not sold, but reporting to the nearest taxation office is one of the formal steps required for brewing beer at home in Germany, and the specific gravity rules are just a part of beer making!

You can only measure the specific gravity of your beer accurately by using a calibrated beer hydrometer. These are available from suppliers of home brewing equipment relatively cheaply. These beer hydrometers are calibrated to 20° C as most hobby brewers use top-fermenting yeast. The hydrometer (see photo on right) is placed in a small amount of wort that has been cooled to fermentation temperature (20° C). The hydrometer sinks, depending on the specific gravity, and the exact gravity can be read on a scale on the top of the hydrometer. You can test the accuracy of the hydrometer by placing it in pure water. At a temperature of 20° C the scale should read exactly zero, as there are no dissolved extracts in pure water.

Conduct repeated tests during fermentation to check its progress.

> As the fermentation process proceeds, and the brewing yeast converts the sugar into alcohol and carbon dioxide, the specific gravity of the wort drops. This is the only way you can determine the end of primary fermentation and thus the correct time to bottle the finished beer.

Frequent checking of the specific gravity is not as vital if you use the speise method, however you must determine that primary fermentation has ended and that is only possible with the beer hydrometer. If your first test reveals a specific gravity of 12 degrees, then approximately 5 degrees is the time to bottle the beer for secondary fermentation. If the finished beer is placed in bottles for secondary fermentation too soon, there is a danger that secondary fermentation will result in over-pressure which could cause the bottles to explode. The forces released during fermentation are tremendous. An exploding bottle acts like a bomb, flinging glass splinters in a radius of several meters, and can pose a threat to people. If the beer is bottled too late, no carbon dioxide is formed during secondary fermentation and without sparkling carbon dioxide the beer tastes flat and can only be "cut" with purchased beer.

Bottle the beer when the specific gravity reaches approximately 5 degrees.

In order to obtain an accurate reading during fermentation, the test sample must be vigorously stirred or shaken to remove the carbon dioxide, otherwise the presence of the gas will result in a false reading.

To remove the carbon dioxide during testing, you can also filter your test sample through a paper coffee filter, which removes the gas. Do not stir with the hydrometer, which is made of glass, as it breaks easily. The simplest beer hydrometer cost between 10 and 15 dollars, and can be purchased from specialty shops or drugstores. There are also significantly more comfortable versions of these testing devices, for example with an integral thermometer and, depending on the size of the hydrometer, a detailed scale.

More elaborate beer hydrometers have integral thermometers.

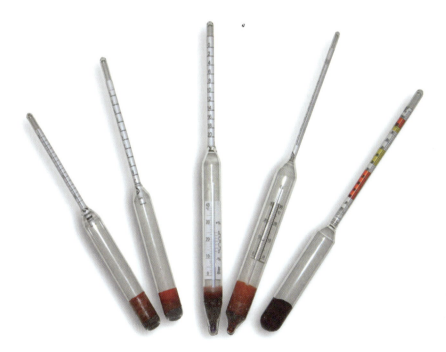

Some hydrometers beer hydrometers have integral thermometers.

Pitching the Yeast and Primary Fermentation

Once the fermentation temperature has been reached, depending on the fermentation method—top- of bottom fermentation—the prepared brewing yeast is added to the cooled wort.

> If dry yeast is used, it must be prepared (reanimated) several hours before it is pitched.

Dry yeast

The dry yeast is added to the quantity of water specified on the package and thus reactivated. To check if the dry yeast is, in fact, active, you can dissolve some sugar in the water. If the yeast is working, bubbles will appear on the surface of the liquid, as fermentation is converting the sugar into carbon dioxide and alcohol. The rising bubbles are a clear indication of this process. With liquid yeast, which you harvested from your last brewing effort and stored in a bottle in the refrigerator, there is no need for the reanimation process as the beer yeast is already in liquid form. You can also test liquid yeast for activity using the same method. The yeast should always be pitched at the optimal fermenting temperature. Top-fermenting yeast from the refrigerator must be warmed slowly to about 20° C.

Dissolved dry yeast

Packaged liquid yeast purchased from brew shops must be activated some time before it is used. Precise information can be found on the packaging. Depending on the kind of yeast, it may be several days before the yeast reaches optimal working conditions.

You should now decide in which fermenting vessel you will carry out the fermentation process. For your first attempts, the clean mash/wort pot will suffice, as its capacity matches your batch size exactly.

> If you intend to brew regularly, it is advantageous to obtain a dedicated fermenting vessel, if possible with an integral spigot on the bottom or side.

Tempered liquid yeast is added to the wort.

Fermentation vessels can be bought from some hardware or farm supply stores where they are sold as "cider casks" or "fruit wine casks." Be absolutely sure that the containers are made of food grade plastic, from which no harmful substances, like cancer-causing chemical solvents, can leach during the fermentation process. These containers come in a variety of styles and sizes, some with plastic spigots others with metal spherical head valves, with a lid into which an airlock can be inserted. With this type of vessel you can ferment in the classical way using an uncovered pail or create a sealed fermenting tank with an air lock to release the pressure. When purchasing such a pail, make sure that it is easy to clean.

Specialty shops offer fermenting tanks for refrigerators which are equipped with carbon dioxide cartridges, making it possible to tap the finished beer from the tank.

These tanks have devices which float on the beer, making it possible to draw clear beer from the surface. The yeast remains on the bottom and is not stirred up when beer is tapped.

It takes several hours for fermentation to commence, during which time the unfermented beer is especially vulnerable to wild yeast or bacteria in the air.

Air lock.
(Photo: www.holzeis.com)

> To give the yeast an optimal start, after the yeast is added the wort is well aerated, meaning well stirred with a cooking spoon, beer paddle, or whisk, in order to raise the oxygen level in the wort as much as possible.

Oxygen is vital for the initiation of fermentation. If wild yeasts gain the upper hand over your pure yeast, the result will be spoiled fermentation, as these wild yeasts, and especially lactic acid bacteria, will overpower the beer yeast. The finished beer will be sour and, thus, undrinkable. Until bubbles form on the surface of the wort, therefore, cover the fermenting tank with a clean cloth or well-fitting cover. The vigorous fermentation that begins after 12-24 hours with top-fermented beer will initially create a layer of white foam (called kräusen), which after a while begins to turn brown because of the dead yeast and hop elements. This foam should carefully be removed from the fermenting pail with a ladle.

> Make sure not to exceed the allowable temperature for top-fermenting yeasts of 15-20° C during primary fermentation.

In addition to alcohol and carbon dioxide, the biological processes during alcoholic fermentation caused by beer yeast also produce thermal energy (heat), which can cause the temperature of the liquid to rise above the optimal fermenting temperature. You can regulate the temperature relatively accurately with refrigerant gel packs or ice-filled soda bottles. If the temperature rises too much during fermentation, you will not have a controlled fermentation and the excessively high temperatures will damage or completely kill the yeast. If fermentation is too strong, the result is significantly more by-products such as esters, which can affect taste and, in cases of excessive consumption, lead to headaches.

Excessively high temperatures during fermentation can harm the yeast.

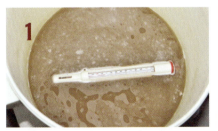

1 and 2: the start of primary fermentation.

3 and 4: primary fermentation.

1: Start of fermentation.
2: Checking temperature.
3: Advanced fermentation.
4: Top-fermenting yeast after
    about 2-3 days.

Fermenting With Top-Fermenting Yeast

Depending on the yeast that is used, the process now taking place takes about two to three days. Particularly active yeasts, especially those that have been used several times, begin primary fermentation very quickly, and the entire primary fermentation process may only take 2 to 2½ days. The exact state of fermentation can only be determined with a beer hydrometer, however. As described in the chapter Measuring Specific Gravity, the gravity of the beer drops as fermentation progresses, while, at the same time, alcohol content rises and the carbon dioxide formed during fermentation escapes into the air.

> Use of the hydrometer will tell you exactly when to end primary fermentation and transfer the beer to bottles or kegs for secondary fermentation.

If the specific gravity of the wort is 12° when the yeast is pitched, then the optimal time for ending the primary fermentation will lie between 5° and 6°. At that point, there is still sufficient sugar present to enrich the beer with carbon dioxide in the bottle or keg during secondary fermentation, and the danger of excessive pressure and the resulting explosion of bottles is eliminated. You have better control over the timing of bottling with the two forms of speise addition described on page 79.

Top-fermenting beer yeasts do not degenerate as quickly as bottom-fermenting yeasts and can be reused many more times for home brewing. The harvested yeast is "washed," meaning it is mixed well with water. After a while the yeast drops to the bottom, the excess yeast is removed from the bottle, leaving just a thin layer of liquid over the yeast, and the bottle is subsequently covered and stored in the refrigerator for later use. The middle third of the yeast is best suited for reuse, as that is where the most active yeast is concentrated. By carefully separating the extracted yeast one can preserve the best cells.

Fermenting With Bottom-Fermenting Yeast

As mentioned in the chapters Brewing at Home and Yeasts, bottom-fermenting require much lower temperatures of 4–8° C for home brewing, something that cannot be achieved all year round at home without electrical cooling. With a little effort and good faith you can find a way, for example by converting an old refrigerator into an electrical cooling system. It is certainly better if you wait until winter to begin your bottom-fermenting beer efforts if it is your intention to achieve and maintain these low temperatures of 4–8° C for a week.

> Whereas the primary fermentation of top-fermenting yeasts takes 2 to 3 days, with bottom-fermenting yeasts it takes considerably longer—more than a week, around 7 to 8 days.

Home brewing suppliers now offer bottom-fermenting yeasts that work satisfactorily at temperatures of 15° C, which makes use of these yeasts at home significantly easier. These yeast strains seek to combine the advantages of both fermentation methods—fermentation without electrical cooling with top-fermenting yeasts and the longer shelf life of bottom-fermented beers.

Fermentation of bottom-fermenting beers is not as vigorous as with top-fermented beers, and the external indications of fermentation, such as the rising of carbon dioxide bubbles, are less obvious.

> Accurate measurements with the hydrometer are vital here in determining the end of primary fermentation.

The long primary fermentation stage of bottom-fermented beers makes it possible to determine the exact time to transfer the beer to bottles or kegs. With top-fermented beers, however, it is possible that the time for bottling has not come by bedtime, but by morning fermentation has progressed so far that secondary fermentation in bottles or kegs cannot be achieved without the addition of sugar. The "speise method" described on page 79 can remedy this situation.

Several German-language books recommend that the so-called "young beer" is siphoned into a glass carboy or other suitable container after primary fermentation to mature and become enriched with carbon dioxide, a process similar to that used by breweries. We do not consider this technically complicated closed system, which is designed to prevent the loss of carbon dioxide from the beer, to be of any use in home brewing. It does simulate closely the beer-brewing process used by the breweries (lagering in fermentation tanks) and filters out much of the sediment and yeast remnants. Overall the beer is made clearer, but without industrial filtering systems it is not possible for the home brewer to filter all of the yeast and sediment from the beer without losing all of the carbon dioxide.

With bottom-fermenting yeasts fermentation is not as vigorous.

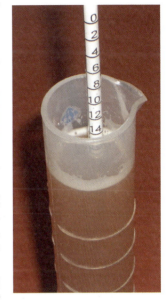

Determining the specific gravity.

Without an industrial filter it is impossible to remove all of the yeast and impurities from the beer.

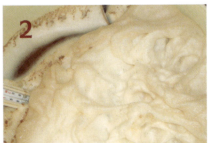

1: Primary fermentation completed.
2: Carefully remove foam with a ladle.
3: Temperature check.
4: Ready for bottling.

We therefore recommend that you follow the example of hobby brewers in England and America and carry out secondary fermentation in bottles. The beer is placed in carefully cleaned bottles as soon as the optimum moment arrives, as determined by the hydrometer.

In this way the bottled beer contains sufficient yeast cells to initiate secondary fermentation in the bottle—provided the sugar content of the young beer is sufficient. The addition of speise gives you a certain amount of time to play with. During secondary fermentation the yeast remnants and sediment sinks to the bottom of the bottle. Through careful pouring the solids remain on the bottom of the bottle and the beer remains clear. You can keep track of and regulate the carbon dioxide pressure by open the bottle several times (swing-top bottle).

Bottling and Aging the Young Beer

There are several ways of aging your beer before drinking, with corresponding advantages and disadvantages. The most widely used method of storing and transporting beer is placing it in beer bottles of various shapes and sizes. Other popular containers are kegs made of aluminum or steel, and less frequently wood, plus cans. With some limitations, all of these options are available to you at home.

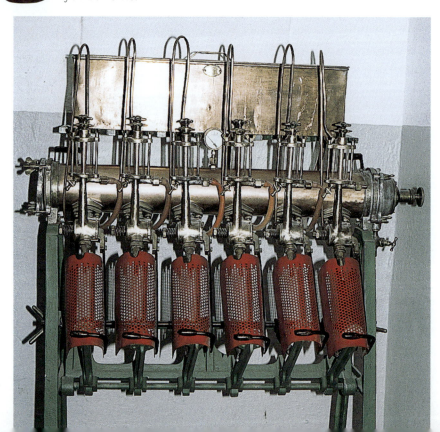

Vintage bottling system.

Bottling

The simplest—and probably also the best suited for the needs of the home brewer—are the swing-top bottles with porcelain caps. These bottles began their triumphal march more than 100 years ago. They were eventually superseded by crown-cap bottles and it has only been in recent years that they have reappeared, mainly in nostalgic bottle shapes for specialty beers. These bottles are commercially available in many sizes and shapes. They all have one thing in common, namely the rubber ring, which forms a seal beneath the porcelain cap and prevents the escape of carbon dioxide. Like all other bottles they are easy to clean, and the rubber rings are sterilized in boiling water or replaced if worn. Swing-top glass bottles are available in sizes from 0.3 to 0.5 liters.

Bottle with porcelain cap.

Returnable glass bottles and the slender NRW bottles can also be used at home, for which you require a bottle capper and an appropriate number of bottle caps. The bottle capper (see illustration) and caps can be obtained from suppliers of home brewing equipment.

Dark bottles are used because of beer's sensitivity to light.

> ### ATTENTION!
>
> Crown caps can only be used once and must be replaced with new caps every time. If you do bottle with crown caps, you must first determine the exact fermentation in order to achieve optimal secondary fermentation in the bottle.

You do not have the option—as with swing-top bottles—of making adjustments to the secondary fermentation process by releasing excess pressure or compensating for too little pressure by adding a small amount of sugar to the bottle.

Not exactly true to the original style, but entirely suitable for bottling beer, are mineral water bottles made of glass and soft drink bottles made of food grade plastic. The caps must be tight enough to prevent the escape of carbon dioxide. You will have to decide for yourself whether you want to serve beer from cola bottles! These bottles do have one important disadvantage, for beer is not placed in dark brown bottles for nothing. It is very light sensitive, therefore these bottles, which are usually clear or white, should not be used to store beer for longer periods.

(Photo: www.holzeis.com)

Kegs

Kegs can also be used to hold your homemade beer, although their use requires much more effort. Wooden kegs are almost never used any more, as few breweries can afford to use this original beer transport and storage system. Wooden kegs are much more difficult to clean than steel or aluminum kegs, and from time to time wooden kegs must be "pitched." This process, which keeps the kegs gas-tight and prevents the escape of carbon dioxide, is time-consuming and expensive. Steel and aluminum kegs are available in sizes suitable for the home brewer (10-12 liters), although they require filling and dispensing systems with CO_2 cartridges. As previously mentioned, there are small plastic kegs with an integral tapping system and carbon dioxide cartridges, which make it possible to store beer longer in the keg and keep it in the refrigerator for several days after it is "tapped."

Another way to store your beer is in small metal party kegs (5 liters). Fitted with a plug in their base, these party kegs are cleaned, the plug is removed, and they are then filled with your beer. You need your own dispensing system, through which air is pumped into the keg or a carbon dioxide cartridge that is used to allow the beer to be tapped. Tapping with a hand pump stirs up the beer yeast, however, making it almost impossible to draw off a clear beer.

Preparation of Containers

No matter which form of container you choose for your beer, proper hygienic preparation of these containers is absolutely vital. As mentioned numerous times, the best method for bottles and kegs is a thorough cleaning with hot water and a bottle brush followed by a rinse in cold water. This method will usually suffice to enable you to store your beer for a lengthy period with no loss of quality.

Beer kegs (above) and various stoppers. (Photo: www.holzeis.com)

Standard dishwashing liquids and dishwasher detergents, most of which contain fat, should not be used to clean beer bottles, cans and kegs, as the fat leaves behind residue.

Fat destroys the surface tension of the water, preventing a proper head from forming on the beer. On the other hand soda, which dissolves in hot water, is suitable for cleaning bottles and kegs. To mechanically improve the effectiveness of the cleaning, the insides of the bottles should also be cleaned with a bottle brush.

The speise, which you took from the wort and have kept in cold storage, now comes into play. Several hours before the end of primary fermentation the bottles with the speise are removed from the refrigerator and placed beside the fermenter in order to raise the speise to fermentation temperature. Before the young beer is bottled, the speise is added to the fermenter, after which bottling can begin at once.

Filling bottles using a juicer.

Bottling using a tube.

Bottling Methods

The bottling of beer is accomplished in various ways, each with its advantages and disadvantages. The most inexpensive method is to use a plastic or rubber tube. One end of the tube is carefully placed in the vessel with the beer, while the other end is sucked on and placed in the bottle. The bottle is then filled to within about 3 centimeters of the top. A hose clamp is used to control the flow of beer. With this method it is advantageous to have a second person to help by ensuring that the end of the tube is always beneath the level of the beer to ensure a continuous flow. Bottles should not be filled too quickly to prevent the excess buildup of foam and associated loss of carbon dioxide.

Bottling is much simpler and easier to regulate if the fermenter is equipped with a spigot. A plastic tube, long enough to reach the bottom of the bottle, is attached to the spigot. One advantage of this method is that you can bottle your beer without help.

Use of this filling method also allows you to better control the flow rate and prevent excessive foaming.

Specialty shops offer inexpensive tube filling systems, which make it possible to fill the bottles with beer from bottom to top, preventing the escape of carbon dioxide.

Today breweries bottle their beer with closed systems, using counter-pressure to prevent the escape of carbon dioxide. You can make a similar system at home, and the results more than justify the financial and technical outlay.

Refillable cans and steel kegs can also be used at home. After thorough cleaning they are filled by means of a tube or spigot in a manner similar to that used with bottles. The cans are filled by means of the opening on the top of the can, which is then sealed with a hard rubber plug. Air locks are available for these cans, making secondary fermentation in the can possible without the danger of over-pressure.

A certain amount of spillage is unavoidable during bottling. Use of a catch basin will help keep the mess to a minimum.

Bottle Labels

If you have a number of different beers from different batches in your cellar or refrigerator, from the outside it is impossible to tell one from the other. To be able to determine the best time to drink your beer, you should at least mark the bottling date on the bottles, cans and kegs. Bottle labels, on the other hand, contain more much information about the bottled beer, such as gravity, alcohol content, the name of the beer, and information about its bottling date and shelf life. Labels on commercial beers also contain other information for advertising and selling purposes.

Given the amount of effort you have put into creating it, you should not shy away from designing labels for your beer. Important information such as the bottling date and name of the beer, at least, belongs on every label.

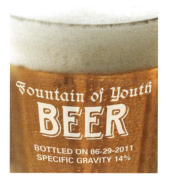

Beer label.

> By creating individual bottle labels, you can turn your homemade beer into a very personal gift for friends and family.

Storing the Finished Beer

While beer placed in bottles or refillable cans is finished and referred to as young beer, it must spend some time in the cellar to mature. During this maturation, which for your beer takes place in the bottle, the beer is enriched with carbon dioxide and flavor components of the beer develop further. The bottles are kept at fermenting temperature for several days for secondary fermentation; in a warm place for top-fermenting beers. The fermenting temperature for bottom-fermented beers is 4 to 8° C, consequently these beers can be placed in cool storage immediately. The excess pressure created during secondary fermentation cannot escape the bottle. Swing-top bottles are therefore ideally suited for the release of possible over-pressure by opening and immediately resealing the cap.

During secondary fermentation the beer is enriched with carbon dioxide.

> Cans and bottles, which are sealed with hard rubber plugs and crown caps respectively, cannot be vented in this way; for this reason a hydrometer must be used to determine the precise moment for bottling, in order to prevent the excessive formation of carbon dioxide in the bottle.

There are many suitable containers for lagering beer.

With experience you can achieve consistent concentrations of carbon dioxide. As in all brewing operations, it is important to keep detailed records in your beer log.

In the first days after primary fermentation you should check the pressure in the filled containers daily, in order to avoid the possible exploding of beer bottles due to excess pressure created during secondary fermentation. If the pressure decreases when the bottle is opened—which is obvious from the sound it makes—it is time to stop venting. A certain amount of residual pressure is absolutely necessary for the shelf life of the beer. If there is no excess pressure on opening the bottle after the first day, fermentation of the beer had already ended and therefore no carbon dioxide can form in the bottled beer. If this is the case, refer to the chapter "Brewing Mistakes" (page 99 ff) for a remedy.

After several days, the top-fermented beer, now enriched with carbon dioxide, can be stored in a cool place. To bring secondary fermentation to a complete finish, it is advantageous to store the beer at a temperature of 2–4° C, which causes the top-fermenting yeast to become inactive.

ATTENTION!

Beer is very light and temperature sensitive! A mildly-alcoholic beverage, beer freezes at a temperature of -2° C and after freezing beer is usually cloudy and has an unpleasant aftertaste. If the beer freezes there is also a danger of bottles bursting.

This brewing mistake is not to be confused with so-called "ice beers" in which the beer is intentionally concentrated by freezing (in breweries) in order to obtain a special flavor and increase alcohol content. Sudden temperature changes damage beer; therefore, the bad habit of rapidly cooling warm beer by placing it in the freezer is not advisable.

8° C is the optimal beer lagering and drinking temperature.

Always store your beer—whether bought or brewed yourself—standing in a dark room at 8° C. This optimal storage temperature is also the best drinking temperature for beer. Stronger beers such as *Bockbiere* (bock beers) and specialty beers can definitely be drunk at higher temperatures, as aromas develop better at somewhat higher temperatures. Light beers and alcohol-reduced beers, on the other hand, are served and consumed colder than 8° C.

Top-fermented beers require a shorter conditioning period in the bottle than bottom-fermented beers and are ready to drink after two weeks. These beers have a shorter shelf life, and should be consumed within 8-10 weeks after conditioning.

The longer the beer remains in the bottle, the clearer it becomes, as the yeast components and turbid matter settle to the bottom of the bottle as sediment. When serving, if the beer is carefully poured into the glass this sediment will remain on the bottle and the beer in the glass will be wonderfully clear. Yeast cells are living organisms and eventually die, which can negatively affect the taste of the beer. In breweries these yeast elements are filtered out of the beer, and beer is often pasteurized by heating to 78° C for better shelf life. These processes turn a living drink ("basis for life") into a totally dead one.

Bottom-fermented beers theoretically have a longer shelf life, but the same applies to these yeasts. Yeast dies, and this can affect the taste of the beer. Bottom-fermented beers only fully develop their aromas after a somewhat longer lagering (storage) period, but they then possess a longer shelf life.

> **RULE OF THUMB:**
>
> The basic principle: the stronger the beer is brewed, the longer it can be stored.

These storage times are only approximate values. "Forgotten" bottles of home brewed beer still had excellent flavor components to offer after a year, and the long storage period had made them completely clear as the sediment was stuck to the bottom of the bottle.

Brewing Log

As mentioned a number of times in this book, you should keep a record of your work steps and operations in the form of a brewing log. On the one hand, this allows you to recognize mistakes that were made and avoid them in future, while, on the other, it allows you to recreate exactly a particularly successful beer. As well, because of tax laws breweries are required to keep records, because specific gravity and output are the basis for the payment of the beer tax, which is based on the quantity and strength of the beer.

The brewing log is used for post calculation and to determine yield during brewing and is thus an important control instrument in recognizing rationalization effects in the breweries.

On page 145, you can see one such brewing log from a small brewery, in which the responsible brew master has made his entries.

Dead yeast cells can negatively affect the flavor of the beer.

You should keep a record of each step and operation in your brewing log.

Brewing Log

The following information should always
be recorded in your brewing log:

- Brewing date

- Quantity of malt used (grain bill),
  the types of malt and the actual mix

- Amount of water added at mashing

- Mashing temperature and rest times

- First saccharification rest (protein rest) with rest time,
  result of iodine test after the rest

- Second saccharification rest with rest time,
  result of iodine test after the rest

- Sparge, i.e., the quantity of water
  used to wash the residual grain

- Type and quantity of hops,
  number of additions

- Wort boiling time

- Type and quantity of yeast pitched,
  temperature at time of pitching

- Time yeast pitched

- Specific gravity when yeast pitched

- Start of primary fermentation
  (formation of bubbles)

- Duration of primary fermentation

- Quantity of speise added

- Bottling date

- Duration of secondary fermentation in bottle

- Start of lagering period in refrigerator

- Space for comments and observations

Such detailed information is not normally necessary for brewing at home, however you should make notes about every brew in order to correctly assign mistakes and improve future brewing efforts.

Just as you should identify your beer with your own labels, you should also create a brew log for each beer or design your own brewing log using photocopies.

Create a separate log for each beer.

Tasting the Finished Beer

If you have made it this far, then the high point of brewing at home now stands before you: tasting your own beer for the first time. Enjoy these moments and ensure that everything can happen under optimal conditions. In the previous section we spoke briefly about the optimal drinking temperature of 8° C. But there is more to the enjoyment of beer than correct temperature alone; there are other factors to take into consideration. The sight alone of a well-tapped beer causes the mouth to water, for we enjoy beer not just with our sense of taste but with all our senses. Opening the bottle lets us know acoustically whether enough carbon dioxide has formed in the bottle. From the smell of the beer after it has been poured we can draw conclusions about the quality of the beer, and a beer with a tall head of foam is pleasing to the eye and causes the heart to beat faster. With our taste buds we can then examine the taste of the beer and compare its quality with bought beer or beer from previous brewing efforts.

After the sediment in your home-brewed beer has clearly settled to the bottom of the bottle, use care when pouring in order to prevent the yeast and other sediments from flowing into the glass.

If the beer was cool-stored for a sufficient period, it will be quite clear and entirely comparable in clarity to commercial beers. Of course by shaking the bottle you can stir up the sediment, as in a *Zwicklbier*, and let it flow into the beer glass. Many breweries now offer such unfiltered *Zwicklbiere* as specialty beers; *Weizenbier* is offered yeast clouded, meaning unfiltered, as *Hefeweizen*.

You should also select a suitable beer glass from the wide variety available. There are special glasses for the various varieties of beer, from *Biertulpen* (literally beer tulips) for pilsners, which retain the head particularly well, to tall wheat beer glasses with wide tops, to small *Altbier* glasses.

Serving beer in an appropriate glass with a nice head enhances the drinking experience.

You should be aware that beer glasses absolutely should not be cleaned with dishwasher detergent, which contains fat, and no fatty liquids such as milk should be drunk from them, as fat residue in the glass will destroy the beer's surface tension and prevent the formation of a good head of foam.

You have surely already seen that good innkeepers rinse beer glasses thoroughly with cold water before drawing a beer in order to remove the last remnants of detergent. Restaurants use special fat-free detergents for cleaning beer glasses which leave behind no residue.

For your glasses at home it will usually suffice to wash them in hot water and then rinse thoroughly with cold water. Then place the glasses on a dish towel with the opening down to drain and let them dry.

In order to form an objective opinion of your home-brewed beer you should not conduct the taste-testing alone, instead you should invite your friends and relatives to sample it and then ask for their honest opinion. A comparison, possibly in the form of a blind taste test with commercial beer, will surely ease the task of evaluating your homemade beer. Such tests will sharpen your senses and help you detect the slight variations in taste that various ingredients give to your beer. Be calmly critical in assessing your beer, but don't allow unjustified, unqualified criticism to discourage you.

There is no THE beer; rather, you should try to brew a beer that meets your personal expectations and tastes good to you. As we all know, everyone's tastes are different.

Brewing Mistakes

Even if you exercise the utmost care and maintain the highest possible hygienic conditions at home, it can happen that your beer does not live up to expectations. As emphasized in the previous chapter, it is therefore absolutely vital that you keep records in order to be able to identify brewing mistakes and if possible avoid them the next time you brew.

Obviously the following list of brewing mistakes is not complete and you could encounter many other reasons for brewing or fermentation errors. The mistakes described here in brief are the most commonly encountered home brewing problems, but only some of them can be rectified with the means available to you at home. You should therefore always follow this rule of thumb: **Prevention is better than cure!**

The overriding principle in brewing, both at home and in a brewery, is to painstakingly maintain hygienic conditions, use the freshest possible ingredients and adhere precisely to the specified rest times at the prescribed temperatures.

The purpose of this chapter is to provide you with guidance as to how to save your beer, in which you have invested so much time and effort, should something go wrong. You should not get the impression, however, that problems constantly arise when brewing beer at home. Some of these tricks do not follow the strict terms of the German Purity Law, we would never advise you to use harmful substances or suggest the use of poisonous chemicals. The breweries also use these more or less allowable tricks to save their beer when problems arise in brewing, although they possess the biochemical knowledge to be able to use chemical substances correctly.

Brewing or fermentation errors are usually caused by a combination of mistakes.

Many brewing and fermentation errors can have more than one cause, and there are various possibilities and combinations of errors, which you should identify and eliminate using your brewing log.

The Beer Does Not Ferment

One of the most commonly encountered fermentation problems is that the cooled beer does not begin to ferment. In a normal fermentation process, fermentation should begin within 12-24 hours, recognizable by a white layer of bubbles on the surface of the liquid. There are a number of reasons why fermentation might not begin within this period:

- Improper mashing, resulting in no fermentable malt sugar.
- Did you perform an iodine test?
- What was the result?
- What was the measured specific gravity?
- Did the wort taste sweet?
- Did you adhere to the specified rest times to allow malt sugar to form?

If no malt sugar has formed, fermentation is impossible.

If no malt sugar formed, the iodine test would be negative and the specific gravity would show that no malt sugar had formed, making fermentation impossible. Such wort is unsuitable for fermentation and can only be discarded.

- The yeast was no longer active. Either the yeast was too old or improperly stored or the wort was too hot when it was added and the yeast was thus killed.
- Did you oxygenate the wort well before pitching the yeast?
- If the specific gravity is too high (over 16°) the result can be yeast shock, resulting in inactive yeast.

If you still have some of the same yeast at home, you can test its viability by dissolving it in some speise or sugar water. Bubbles should form on the surface after a time. You can use this yeast for fermentation if only the yeast is involved. If the wort has been sitting for some time without fermentation beginning, it is recommended that before adding fresh yeast you once more bring it to a boil, again sterilizing it, then cool the wort, oxygenate well and add the yeast.

> ■ The presence of too many suspended solids in the wort can suppress fermentation or result in incomplete fermentation.

The wort can be brought to fermentation by once again filtering the wort through a clean cloth diaper and adding fresh yeast. Again, it is recommended that you boil the wort again to sterilize it, cool it and oxygenate the wort well before adding yeast.

Inadequate cleanliness can also cause infections in the wort, which can hinder or prevent fermentation.Boiling the wort again sterilizes it (once again, cool the wort and oxygenate well before pitching the yeast), and adding fresh yeast can result in normal fermentation.

Test your yeast for viability using some speise or water-sugar solution.

Unsanitary working conditions can result in contamination of the wort.

The Finished Beer Tastes Bitter

> ■ Beer that is too bitter is usually the result of adding too much hops or using hops that are too intense.

Note the bitter substances of the hops and record them in your brewing log.

Hop pellets and liquid hop extract are almost twice as intense as dried natural hops. Use less hops in your next brewing sessions and make corresponding notes in your brewing log. Hard water can also cause bitterness in beer. With hard water requires significantly less hops for the same effect as does soft water. You can make bitter beer more enjoyable by cutting it with commercial beer on a 1:1 ratio. Another possibility is to use the beer to make "Radler" by adding fruit juice or lemonade.

The Finished Beer Tastes Too Malty

■ If you add too few hops the beer will taste more malty.

Add liquid hops to
make excessively-malty
beer drinkable.

You can also make this beer drinkable by cutting with commercial beer.

Another remedy is to add liquid hops, either in the bottle or several drops in the finished beer.

ATTENTION! | Liquid hops are very intense!

If the second saccharification rest was too long, too much dextrin formed. This gives the beer body and mellowness, but can also make it taste sweet, as dextrin is not a fermentable sugar. Reduce the duration of the saccharification rest (brewing log).

The Finished Beer Tastes Sour

Do not use
vinegar-based cleaners.

■ One of the most common problems in the fermenting of beer is that the finished beer tastes sour. The cause is usually lactic acid bacteria or, less frequently, vinegar bacteria has prevailed over the pure yeast you added to the wort.

Wort infected with vinegar fungus during primary fermentation.

"Wild yeast" present in the air can also very often prevail against these pure yeasts. The cause and trigger of contamination by these wild yeasts and bacteria can be contaminated fermentation equipment and vessels. Always ensure to maintain proper hygienic conditions. Do not use any vinegar-based cleaners.

The "sour beer" problem cannot be rectified, therefore, the finished beer is spoiled. If you notice that your beer is slightly sour, you can "make" a *Berliner Weiße* by adding fruit juice. Mixing with lemonade can also "cover up" these taste limitations and at least make the beer drinkable. Sour beer is not harmful! By adding mother of vinegar (which causes alcohol to turn into vinegar) you can make the sour beer into beer vinegar. All of the alcohol is turned into vinegar in the second alcoholic fermentation.

The Beer Contains Too Little or No Carbon Dioxide

Natural carbon dioxide gives beer its refreshing, sparkling taste. If natural carbon dioxide is absent the beer tastes less refreshing and flat. There are several causes for the loss of carbon dioxide, which can occur at various points during the brewing process.

- Carbon dioxide can escape from the beer if the bottles are filled too quickly.

By carefully filling the bottles, this error can be avoided in the future. Make sure that the tube reaches the bottom of the bottle, and fill it from bottom to top.

If speise is used, sufficient carbon dioxide should form in the bottle during secondary fermentation. Increase the amount of speise if there is insufficient carbon dioxide (brewing log).

The use of speise should result in the formation of sufficient carbon dioxide.

If you notice that no more carbon dioxide is forming in the bottles during secondary fermentation, you can add a teaspoon of sugar per bottle. Of course the addition of sugar is not in accord with the strict conditions of the German Purity Law, but you can use it too enrich your beer with carbon dioxide, and that is the most important thing. You must keep the bottles at fermentation temperature for one to two days—15-20° C for top-fermented beers and 4-8° C for bottom-fermented beers.

> **ATTENTION!**
>
> When adding sugar the bottles must be closed again quickly to prevent foaming over (rising of the yeast).

- Carbon dioxide can escape if the rubber seals of your swing-top bottles are worn or the wire of the cap exerts insufficient pressure to effectively seal the bottle.

New rubber seals can solve this problem. By bending the wire bracket back to its original shape one can increase pressure on the mouth of the bottle and prevent carbon dioxide from escaping.

New rubber rings or bending of the wire bracket can prevent the escape of carbon dioxide.

In addition to the above measures, you can mix the beer without carbon dioxide with commercial beer in order to make it drinkable.

Too Much Carbon Dioxide in The Beer

> ■ Too much carbon dioxide can form in beer if primary fermentation was not complete (what was the measured specific gravity on bottling day?), and subsequent secondary fermentation produces excess pressure.

Excess pressure in the bottle means that primary fermentation is not yet completed.

The high pressure creates the danger of exploding bottles. Such bottles are proper bombs, and flying pieces of glass can pose a threat to people.

If, when bleeding the beer bottles, you notice that the pressure in the bottles is too great, it usually means that primary fermentation was not complete and that the beer continued to ferment in the bottles and produced excess pressure. Contamination in the bottles can also result in active fermentation in the bottles.

A certain amount of pressure should remain in the bottle, however, as carbon dioxide has a preservative effect.

By carefully opening and immediately closing the swing-top bottles, it is possible to bleed off this excess pressure. Use caution when opening the bottles to avoid being sprayed in the face with beer! In the beginning, when the overpressure is greatest, the bottles should be bled daily. When the pressure decreases, switch to bleeding every second day. A certain amount of pressure should be able to form in the bottle to enrich the beer with carbon dioxide, which also acts as a preservative and keeps it from spoiling. You can also empty all the bottles back into the bottling bucket and fill them again. This time be sure to check the specific gravity first.

> If you worked with speise, the quantity used—relative to the amount of brew—can be too great. Note this in your brewing log and next time reduce the amount of speise.

Other Brewing Mistakes

Most problems are caused by a lack of cleanliness.

The mistakes described here are the most commonly encountered ones. Of course, there are many other mistakes and combinations of brewing and fermenting errors, however, to describe them all would exceed the scope of this book.

> Summarizing, it can be said that most home brewing mistakes are the result of inadequate hygiene, poor malt or bad brewing yeast, and that you can influence and change very few of them.

It is of course unfortunate if the results of your brewing efforts are partially or completely wrecked by these environmental influences, but on the other hand these problems do not always arise and one learns from these mistakes.

The New Beer Brewing Machines

by Ing. Michael Holzeis

In recent times technically complex but time-saving "automatic brewing machines" have become commercially available.

These micro breweries are ideal for someone who is a bit more technical and less labor-intensive but desires to be truly independent. At the same time they are less likely to result in spills and the associated cleaning of the work area. Spare time is already in short supply.

The following is a brief look at the two devices presently on the market for hobby brewers. A new chapter has been added to this successful handbook to include these machines, which undeniably expand the possibilities open to the home brewer, and provide you the reader with basic technical information and illustrations.

Both devices use processor control and two different "stirring methods" to complete the brewing process almost fully automatically. For several years I have personally put both of these excellent machines through their paces and would like to share my experiences with the reader.

The Speidel Company's "Braumeister" (left).

The Brumas Company's "BrauEule®" (right).

Programming the controller

Braumeister®
(circulating infusion mash process)

Controls

An elaborate, menu-guided computer control system greatly simplifies and largely automates the brewing process normally carried out with a thermometer and stopwatch. Before beginning, a pre-programmed "brewing automatic" reviews all the standard recipe parameters. These are optimized to the standard brewing malts available on the hobby brewing market. Happily for the hobbyist, Braumeister does not limit creativity. At any time one can program his own recipe parameters to create the beer of his choice. The entire program is accompanied by a text menu which tells the hobby brewer what to do.

Mashing

Mashing

About 20-25 liters of brewing water are added. This is simplified by markings on the machine. When the water has reached the necessary temperature (e.g., 38° C), a "malt tube," seen here in the center of the brew pot, is inserted and sealed at the bottom by means of rubber lips (see photo). The mash is trapped between two strainer inserts, forming a sort of filter cartridge. This entire section virtually forms a pot within a pot connected to the larger pot by means of a pump.

Brewing (Decoction) Process

As a result of pumping (an old American hobby brewing process, similar to the RIM process), the mash is continuously flushed at the correct temperature and the desired ingredients are exposed to enzymes and released. Concentric heating coils maintain temperature very well. Both actual and target temperatures are shown on the display.

Brewing in progress

Lautering

The program stops and a loud beep indicates that it is time to lauter. Using his strong hands or the optional hand pulley block system, the hobby brewer raises the malt tube with mash, then grist, from the larger pot and fixes it in place using the U-shaped insert. The lautering process begins. Sparging is also possible at this stage.

Lautering

Boiling the Wort and Hops

The wort can be boiled in the Braumeister with pellets or raw hops. Time and temperature are controlled. A visually appealing accessory is a copper cover, which saves energy and can also be used as a vapor exhaust. An optional neoprene thermometer cuff enhances the effect considerably.

Fermentation

Using the stainless steel Wort Cooler accessory the wort is cooled to a temperature of 25-30° C in 15 to 25 minutes.

From then on, everything happens as usual: prepared yeast is added to the still slightly warm wort and fermentation can begin.

Bottle fermentation takes place as usual in pressure-proof bottles or other suitable containers.

The Braumeister is available with nominal volumes of 20, 50 and 200 liters.

Boiling the wort and hops

BrauEule®
(Infusion and decoction mash methods
with steam heating and automatic agitator)

Looking like a miniature "real" brewery, the process is somewhat different than the one just described.

Controls

The BrauEule (literally "Brewing Owl") is also controlled by a sophisticated industrial control system, which, with just four buttons, provides extensive and easily understandable menu navigation. As with the Braumeister, the program can be interrupted at any time and the brewing process resumed at a later time. Very useful in the event of a power failure!

Mashing/Wort Boiling

Mashing and boiling are done in the external stainless steel mash pan (also available in polished copper look).

The difference: steam produced in the main kettle and fed into the external mash pan "stirs" and heats the mash. This eliminates the need for an expensive agitator with its sensitive mechanism. The steam is immediately condensed, eliminating its excessive and annoying release. A temperature sensor assists the control system in adhering to rest times.

Fermentation

Programming the controller

Mashing and …

... boiling the wort

Lautering

Boiling the hops and wort/ hot break separation

Lautering

Separating the wort from the mash is simple and comfortable: simply remove the steam/heat tube and place it in the main boiling kettle, which now becomes the wort pot. Lautering begins and clear wort flows into the pot. Sparging, as usual, is possible.

Hop Boil/Hot Break Separation
(using copper hood)

A special feature of this device is the integrated whirlpool like those in the "real" big breweries.

As may be seen here, this provides for a natural separation of the protein and hop residues. After a night of cooling in hermetically-sealed condition (copper hood) the finished wort can be transferred to the fermentation vessel.

Fermentation

Fermentation takes place as usual.

The BrauEule has a nominal volume of 34 liters. Up to 40 liters of beer can be brewed per batch.

Conclusion

Happily these machines are anything but gadgets. Instead they are practical tools for hobby brewers, as the references show, and also for professionals. Many have already used them to begin successful pub breweries. Even larger private breweries swear by the two machines, using them as efficient and resource-sparing tools to test brews and recipes in their laboratories.

Basic Beer Recipes

Malt Extract Beer
(top-fermented beer)

Ingredients for 15 liters of beer
1 liter   liquid malt extract
15 liters   water
40 grams   hops (pellets)
Dry or liquid yeast (top-fermenting)

This recipe uses liquid malt extract, which you can buy in cans or glass containers. This eliminates the entire mashing and lautering processes. There is also no need for an iodine test, as the malt is already saccharified.

Bring the water to a boil, stirring well to dissolve the liquid malt. Then add the specified quantity of hops and boil the wort for 1½ hours. Filter, cool quickly and pitch the yeast.

Time requirement 2-3 hours.

The advantage of this recipe is its simplicity and small expenditure of time. After completing this first recipe you will surely be stimulated to make the move to "real" beer brewing.

Weizenbock
(top-fermented beer)

Ingredients for 10 liters of beer
1.5 kg   pale malt (Munich)
1.5 kg   wheat malt
20 g   hops (pellets)
8 liters   water
Sparge   8 liters of water
Dry or liquid yeast (top-fermenting)

Ingredients for 20 liters of beer
3 kg   pale malt (Munich)
3 kg   wheat malt
40 g   hops (pellets)
14 liters water
Sparge   12-14 liters of water
Dry or liquid yeast (top-fermenting)

Mash-in at 40° C
Protein rest at 55° C (15 min.)
Raise temperature to 65° C
40 min, saccharification rest (iodine test!)
Raise temperature to 72° C
30 min. final saccharification rest (iodine test!)
Raise temperature to 78° C
30 min. rest, then lauter
*Sparge with 78° C water to wash the
residual sugar from the mash*

*Because of its high alcohol content,
this is a beer for festive occasions.*

Specific gravity approx. 16%
Lagering time 6-8 weeks.

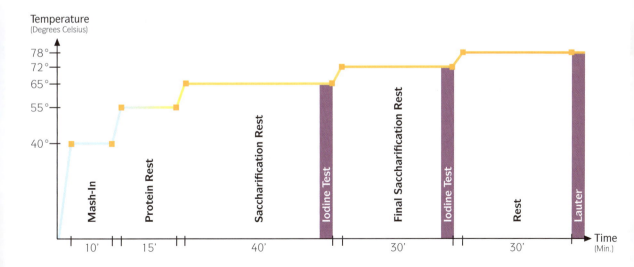

Pilsner
(bottom-fermented beer)

Ingredients for 10 liters of beer
2.3 kg   pale malt
25 g   hops (pellets)
8 liters   water
Sparge   4-6 liters of water
Dry or liquid yeast (bottom-fermenting)

Ingredients for 20 liters of beer
4.5 kg   pale malt
50 g   hops (pellets)
14 liters water
Sparge   6-8 liters of water
Dry or liquid yeast (top-fermenting)

Mash-in at 35° C
Protein rest at 55° C (10 min.)
Raise temperature to 65° C, 30 min.
Saccharification rest (iodine test!)
Raise temperature to 72° C
30 min. final saccharification rest (iodine test!)
Raise temperature to 78° C
30 min. rest, then lauter
Sparge with 78° C water to wash
the residual sugar from the mash

A beer with a hoppy, bitter note.

Specific gravity at least 12%
Lagering time 4-5 weeks.

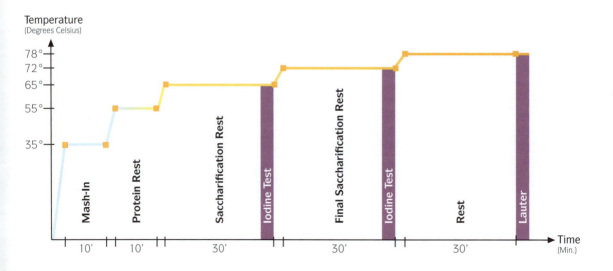

European
Specialty Beers

In this part of the book we have tried to select regionally typical beers that reflect the character and beer culture of each country. We also give you a brief overview of the beer tradition of these countries with curiosities, but without making any claims to completeness.

All of the beers in the recipe section are made with the infusion method, which is the simplest to use in home brewing. All of these beers can of course be made using the decoction method, in which case we would refer you to the Decoction Method section on page 71. In addition to the recipe, you will find information as to whether the beer is top- or bottom-fermented. Suppliers of brewing equipment now offer a wide variety of malt mixtures, which come pre-mixed or unmixed, crushed or whole. Nevertheless you will not always receive the 100% correct malt for each recipe as used in the beer's country of origin. The same, of course, applies to brewing yeast. Some breweries have patented their yeasts and therefore they are rarely available to you for brewing at home. You must therefore make do with the raw materials available to you, to say nothing of optimal brewing water and the various hop mixtures and their influence on the flavor of the finished beer. **But don't let yourself get discouraged, and make the best of the raw materials at your disposal!**

Belgium

No other country in Europe has such a diversity of beer varieties as Belgium. More than 800 different specialty beers are offered in Belgium today, and the associated beer culture is as important to Belgians as wine is to the French. This beer culture is not new but has grown historically, as it has absorbed many influences from neighboring beer countries like Germany, but also from Great Britain. Cooking with beer has a long tradition in Belgium and the flavor nuances that are achieved with these beers are amazing.

One very special specialty beer is lambic, which is brewed using spontaneous fermentation without the addition of cultured yeast. These specialty beers have their origins in the days before brewers learned how to use yeast in making beer.

The sour taste of these beers produced through spontaneous fermentation is not to everyone's taste, however, and it is actually not comparable to the beers we know in Germany. The addition of fruit, mainly cherries, raspberries, and strawberries, to wheat beer produces unusual but very enjoyable flavor variations. Even if these additives do not comply with the German Purity Law, they are natural products that pass their flavorings, sugar, and fruit acids to the mash during the mashing process.

Many of these Belgian specialty beers are top-fermented, and consequently secondary fermentation in the bottle becomes of quite special importance. The five Belgian monastery breweries in Belgium, and one in the neighboring Netherlands, brew Trappist beer, which undergoes secondary fermentation in the bottle using the *champenoise* method. Candy sugar is added during the mashing process and once again during bottling to produce secondary fermentation. This champagne method results in the formation of a visible layer of sediment on the bottom of the bottle.

Belgian wheat beers differ from their German relatives in that crushed unmalted wheat is used instead of wheat malt. You can also use this for brewing at home, especially if no malted wheat malt is available.

In addition to these region-typical varieties, many English-style beers—ales, stouts and porters—are also made in Belgium.

Like some Germans and Czechs, the Belgians consider Gambrinus to be the patron saint of beer. The name Gambrinus probably comes from John I, Duke of Brabant, who lived in present-day Belgium in the 13th century. The name Gambrinus is derived from his Latin name, Jan Primus.

Trappist Beer
(top-fermented beer)

Ingredients for 10 liters of beer
3 kg   pale malt (Pilsner malt)
200 g   candy sugar
20 g   natural hops (Saaz)
8 liters   water
Sparge   8-10 liters of water
Dry or liquid yeast (top-fermenting)

Ingredients for 20 liters of beer
6 kg   pale malt (Pilsner malt)
400 g   candy sugar
40 g   natural hops (Saaz)
13 liters water
Sparge   12-14 liters of water
Dry or liquid yeast (top-fermenting)

Mash-in at 35° C
Protein rest at 55° C (20 min.)
Raise temperature to 65° C
30 min. saccharification rest (iodine test!)
Raise temperature to 72° C
30 min. final saccharification rest (iodine test!)
Raise temperature to 78° C
30 min. rest, then lauter
Sparge with 78° C water to wash
the residual sugar from the mash

Boil with the hops. Divide hops into 2-3 additions.
Dried natural hops from Saaz. Filter and cool,
then pitch the top-fermenting yeast.

Fermentation time 3 days.
Add candy sugar and fresh yeast to the bottles
for secondary fermentation.
Lagering time 6-10 weeks.

This Trappist beer is a particularly strong, pale top-fermented specialty beer which is brewed in the five monastery breweries in Belgium and one in the neighboring Netherlands. Only a beer brewed in one of these Trappist breweries can be called a Trappist beer. Pale Pilsner malt is used for making these beers, as are the same hop varieties used in pilsners. A special feature is the addition of candy sugar to the mash during brewing. A small amount of candy sugar is also used for secondary fermentation in the bottle. Fresh yeast is also added. Because of the addition of sugar and yeast, these bottles obviously have to be purged.

Because of its high specific gravity and alcohol content, this beer also requires a relatively long maturation period to achieve its full flavor, which is unusual for a top-fermented beer.

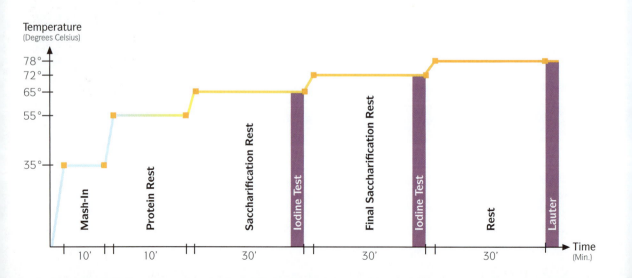

Belgian Wheat Beer – Lambic Beer
(top-fermented beer) – **Lambic Beer**

Ingredients for 10 liters of beer
3 kg	pale malt
1 kg	wheat (unmalted)
25 g	natural hops (pellets)
8 liters	water
Sparge	8-9 liters of water
Dry or liquid yeast (top-fermenting)	

Ingredients for 20 liters of beer
3 kg	pale malt
2 kg	wheat (unmalted)
45 g	natural hops (pellets)
14 liters	water
Sparge	10-12 liters of water
Dry or liquid yeast (top-fermenting)	

Mash-in at 45° C
Protein rest at 55° C (15 min.)
Raise temperature to 65° C
30 min. saccharification rest (iodine test!)
Raise temperature to 72° C
30 min. final saccharification rest (iodine test!)
Raise temperature to 78° C
30 min. rest, then lauter
Sparge with 78° C water to wash
the residual sugar from the mash

Boil with the hops. Divide hops into 2 additions.
Filter and cool, then pitch the top-fermenting yeast.

Fermentation time 2-3 days.
Lagering time 4-6 weeks.

As this wheat beer is brewed with unmalted grain, ensure that the unmalted wheat, which is heavier than malt, does not settle to the bottom of the mash pot. The unmalted wheat also contains no enzymes for breaking down the starch into malt sugar and dextrin, therefore the enzymes in the barley malt must also convert the starch in the wheat. This is, of course, only possible if the barley malt contains sufficient active enzymes, therefore it should be freshly crushed. By definition, a Lambic beer must contain at least 30% unmalted wheat, the rest being barley malt. In Belgium, these beers are normally fermented using spontaneous fermentation, meaning without the addition of cultured yeast. We cannot recommend this method for home brewing, as the results are completely beyond one's control. In Belgium, fruits such as cherries, raspberries, and strawberries are added to wheat beer to achieve special flavor nuances. The beer described above can serve as the basis for these fruit beers, which, with their slightly sour taste, are not everyone's cup of tea. Geuze is a mixture of young and old Lambic beers which undergoes secondary fermentation in the bottle like champagne and also tastes quite sour.

   Fermentation of these wheat beers produces quite a lot of carbon dioxide, which must be vented accordingly by opening the bottles several times.

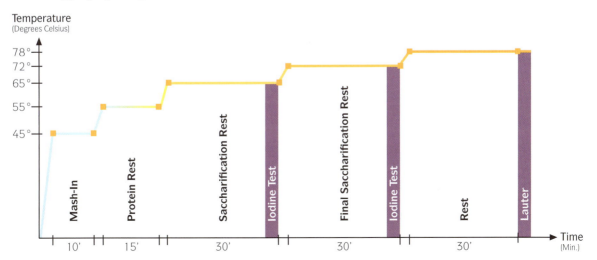

Germany

Nowadays, the Federal Republic of Germany is considered the classic beer nation of central Europe, a claim that will not be debated here. While the process for making bottom-fermented beer was developed in Kleinschwechat near Vienna, and the Czechs today drink more beer than the average German consumer, the influence of the German Purity Law of 1516 explains why Germans are so proud of their beer and why they have fought so hard—unfortunately without success—to retain this law. Many other members of the EU view this law, which is intended primarily to improve beer quality, as unwarranted interference with free trade and a measure that skews competition within the economic community. The waves in this matter have since calmed a little, and many brewing companies that want to serve the German market are voluntarily brewing their beer according to the strict guidelines of the German Purity Law despite the EU rules. The provisions of the law do not include all of the raw materials used in brewing, for in 1516 it was not known that yeast was responsible for alcoholic fermentation, therefore by strict interpretation the addition of cultured yeast would also not be permissible! Many regulations, such as the Austrian Food Code and the Swiss Food Law, are much more restrictive than the pertinent provisions of the German Beer Tax Law. Despite everything, the German Purity Law reflects the beer understanding of the German particularly well, and many brewers in the EU use these regulations as their example; brewing according to the German Purity Law is used as a selling point, especially if they wish to offer their beer on the German market.

> The majority of beers made in Germany today are bottom-fermented varieties—pilsner style or lager and export beers. In many small towns with local breweries, however, local specialty beers are holding their own against their bigger competitors.

There is not just one specialty beer; rather there are a number of styles—not surprising given the size of the market—which we wish to acknowledge in this book. Today, after the reunification of Germany, there are more than 1,300 breweries in the country. In addition to the more popular varieties of beer, these also offer a large number of local and regional specialty beers.

In terms of the number of breweries, the Federal Republic is the undisputed world leader. Approximately 40% of all the breweries in the world are found in this European nation. A real treasure trove of such regional specialties can be found in the Franconia area of Bavaria. Small breweries producing beers characteristic of the area and region have been able to survive in almost every town. Most of these small breweries supply just the inns in the town or, in extreme cases, are operated as pub breweries and thus follow the increasingly popular trend towards small tavern breweries.

Called *Weißbier* in the south of Germany and *Weizenbier* in the north, wheat beer is a specialty beer which falls outside the strict terms of the German Purity Law. A specialty beer from the Berlin area, *Berliner Weiße* is another beer in which is brewed using wheat in malted form in addition to barley malt. In the Munich area there is also the dark, bottom-fermented Munich Style beer, which is rather weakly hopped with malty overtones. Munich is often wrongly identified as the beer capital of Germany, but despite the *Oktoberfest* and the associated consumption of beer, Dortmund is the country's leading beer metropolis. The beers produced there are pale, more strongly hopped, export beers, which also have a somewhat higher specific gravity. Not to be overlooked are the local specialties such as *Kölsch* from Cologne, a pale, top-fermented beer which can only be made in Cologne and which is covered by Protected Designation of Origin, top-fermented *Altbiere* from Frankfurt, Münster, and Hanover, comparable to English ales, *Rauchbiere* from the Bamberg area, made with malt kilned over open an open beech-wood fire, and *Steinbiere*. Then, of course, there are the north-German pilsners, which are extremely dry and very strongly hopped. They differ clearly from the beers of the same name from Pilsen in the Czech Republic, but have already created their own pilsner culture. In the north these pilsners are served in small (0.2 to 0.3 liter) glasses, whereas in Bavaria steins with a capacity of a liter or more—but also sometimes much smaller—are very common, and not just in Munich during *Oktoberfest*.

Many of these beers are suitable for brewing at home and we have decided to provide a more detailed description of several of these specialty beers on the following pages.

Weizenbier
(Wheat Beer, top-fermented)

Ingredients for 10 liters of beer
1 kg   pale malt
1.5 kg   wheat malt
25 g   hops (pellets)
8 liters water
Sparge   8-9 liters of water
Dry or liquid yeast (top-fermenting)

Mash-in at 40° C
Protein rest at 55° C (15 min.)
Raise temperature to 65° C
30 min, saccharification rest (iodine test!)
Raise temperature to 72° C
30 min. final saccharification rest (iodine test!)
Raise temperature to 78° C
30 min. rest, then lauter

Ingredients for 20 liters of beer
2 kg   pale malt
3 kg   wheat malt
45 g   hops (pellets)
14 liters water
Sparge   10-12 liters of water
Dry or liquid yeast (top-fermenting)

Boil with hops. Divide hops into two additions.
Filter and cool and then add the top-fermenting yeast.

Fermenting time 2-3 days.
Lagering time 3-4 weeks.

This wheat beer has an specific gravity of about 12°. Lagering time is 2-3 weeks. Be careful when lagering wheat beer. A relatively large quantity of carbon dioxide forms in the bottle during secondary fermentation, which must be bled off.

The making of beer with unmalted wheat or wheat malt certainly has a long tradition. In 1567, brewing with wheat was forbidden in Bavaria in order to ensure that a suffering population could be fed in the event of a poor harvest. The Bavarian dukes subsequently took advantage of this ban to reserve the brewing of wheat beer to themselves as a state monopoly.

For a long time it appeared that wheat beers would be replaced by new varieties of beer, especially the bottom-fermented lagers and pilsners. It has only been in recent years that this ancient, top-fermented beer has enjoyed a resurgence. Today it is available in two forms: clear *Kristall-* or *Champagnerweißbier* and yeast-clouded *Hefeweißbier*, light or dark. There is also *Weizenbock*, a stronger type of wheat beer.

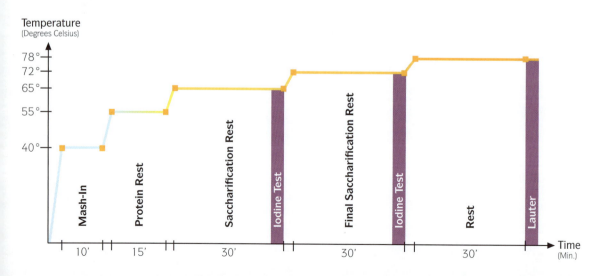

Dunkles Weizenbier
(Dark Wheat Beer, top-fermented)

Ingredients for 10 liters of beer

1.5 kg	pale malt
250 g	caramel malt
25 g	chocolate malt
1.3 kg	wheat malt
20 g	hops (pellets)
8 liters	water
Sparge	8-10 liters of water
Dry or liquid yeast (top-fermenting)	

Mash-in at 35° C
Protein rest at 55° C (15 min.)
Raise temperature to 65° C
40 min, saccharification rest (iodine test!)
Raise temperature to 72° C
30 min. final saccharification rest (iodine test!)
Raise temperature to 78° C
30 min. rest, then lauter
Sparge with 78° C water to wash
the residual sugar from the mash

Ingredients for 20 liters of beer

2.5 kg	pale malt
0.5 kg	caramel malt
50 g	chocolate malt
2.5 kg	wheat malt
30 g	hops (pellets)
16 liters	water
Sparge	16-18 liters of water
Dry or liquid yeast (top-fermenting)	

Boil with hops. Divide hops into two additions.
Filter and cool and then add the top-fermenting yeast.

Fermenting time about 2-3 days.
Lagering time 3-4 weeks.

This dark wheat beer has an specific gravity of about 12°. As for pale wheat beer, lagering time is about 2-3 weeks. This wheat beer is especially well-suited for home brewing, on the one hand because the raw materials can be obtained by mail order relatively easily, and on the other because the top-fermenting method used to make it is the easiest to accomplish at home. And because some commercially-brewed wheat beers are yeast-clouded, the taste of your home-brewed beer is most likely to be similar to that of bought beer. We can heartily recommend these wheat beers for first brewing attempts.

Wheat beers tend to form more carbon dioxide, but they are more refreshing and thirst-quenching, have a slightly sour taste and formerly were drunk mainly during the warmer times of the year. In recent years, the bad habit of putting lemon peel in wheat beer has, thank God, disappeared from the food service industry. For yeast-clouded wheat beers, such as those you make at home, the addition of lemon slices is a totally pointless "flavor enrichment."

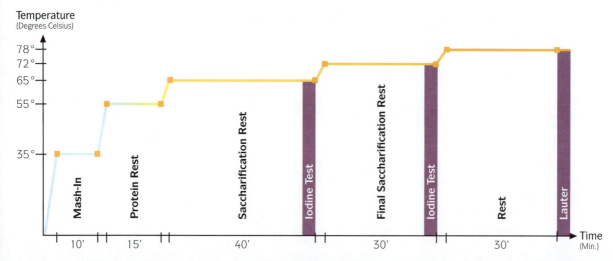

Altbier
(top-fermented beer)

Ingredients for 10 liters of beer

0.5 kg	pale malt
2 kg	dark malt
25 g	hops (pellets)
8 liters	water
Sparge	8 liters of water
Dry or liquid yeast (top-fermenting)	

Ingredients for 20 liters of beer

1 kg	pale malt
4 kg	dark malt
50 g	hops (pellets)
14 liters	water
Sparge	10-12 liters of water
Dry or liquid yeast (top-fermenting)	

Mash-in at 40° C
Protein rest at 55° C (15 min.)
Raise temperature to 65° C
40 min, saccharification rest (iodine test!)
Raise temperature to 72° C
40 min. final saccharification rest (iodine test!)
Raise temperature to 78° C
20 min. rest, then lauter
Sparge with 78° C water to wash
the residual sugar from the mash

Boil with hops. Divide hops into two additions.
Filter and cool and then add the top-fermenting yeast.

Fermenting time 2-3 days.
Lagering time 3-4 weeks.

Specific gravity is about 12°. Lagering time is about 6 weeks. The name *Altbier* (literally "old beer") arises from the fact that this beer is brewed in a traditional, or old, method. This beer is most comparable to English ales or Belgian beers, which are also top-fermented. With its characteristic dark color, *Altbier* is drunk from special small glasses (0.2 liter) and has recently enjoyed renewed popularity as a specialty beer.

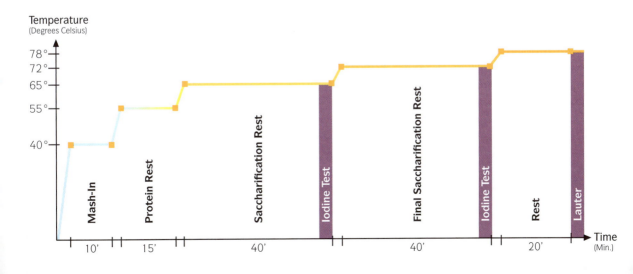

Weizenbock Hell and Dunkel
(top-fermented beer)

Ingredients for 10 liters of beer

1.5 kg	pale malt (Munich mixture)
1.5 kg	wheat malt
20 g	hops (pellets)
8 liters	water
Sparge	8 liters of water
Dry or liquid yeast (top-fermenting)	

Mash-in at 40° C
Protein rest at 55° C (15 min.)
Raise temperature to 65° C
40 min, saccharification rest (iodine test!)
Raise temperature to 72° C
30 min. final saccharification rest (iodine test!)
Raise temperature to 78° C
30 min. rest, then lauter
Sparge with 78° C water to wash
the residual sugar from the mash

Ingredients for 20 liters of beer

3 kg	pale malt (Munich mixture)
3 kg	wheat malt
40 g	hops (pellets)
14 liters	water
Sparge	12-14 liters of water
Dry or liquid yeast (top-fermenting)	

Boil with hops. Divide hops into two to three additions.
Filter and cool and then add the top-fermenting yeast.

Fermenting time about 3 days.
Lagering time 8-10 weeks.

The specific gravity of this beer, which is brewed for special occasions, is approximately 16°. Unlike other bock beers, which are usually brewed at Christmas or Easter, in Bavaria this *Weizenbock* is offered in spring as *Maibock*. Brewing *Weizenbock* at home requires some knowledge and skill in order to prevent the yeast from suffering from yeast shock on account of the high alcohol content.

The name *Bock* does not come from the word *Ziegenbock* (billy goat), as is wrongly held and claimed by many beer labels; rather it is the result of a distortion of the word "Einbeck"—a city in Lower Saxony that was and is known for its strong beer.

By adding 0.5 kg (1 kg for 20 liters) of dark caramel malt and 30 g of chocolate malt (50 g for 20 liters) you can also brew a dark *Weizenbock* at home using the recipe above.

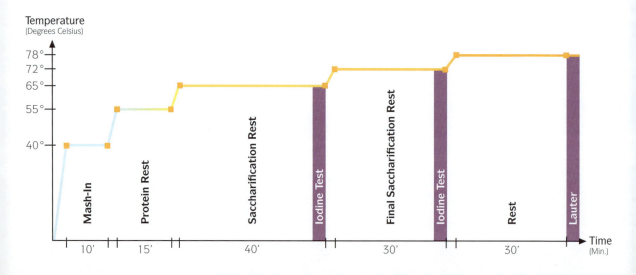

"Kölsch"
(top-fermented beer)

Ingredients for 10 liters of beer
2.2 kg   pale malt
30 g   Hallertauer hops (pellets)
8 liters water
Sparge   4-6 liters of water
Dry or liquid yeast (top-fermenting)

Ingredients for 20 liters of beer
4.3 kg   pale malt
50 g   Hallertauer hops (pellets)
14 liters water
Sparge   6-8 liters of water
Dry or liquid yeast (top-fermenting)

Mash-in at 35° C
Protein rest at 55° C (10 min.)
Raise temperature to 65° C
30 min, saccharification rest (iodine test!)
Raise temperature to 72° C
30 min. final saccharification rest (iodine test!)
Raise temperature to 78° C
30 min. rest, then lauter
Sparge with 78° C water to wash
the residual sugar from the mash

Boil with hops. Divide hops into two to three additions.
Filter and cool and then add the top-fermenting yeast.

Fermenting time about 2-3 days.
Lagering time 4-6 weeks.

There are more breweries in Cologne than in any other city in Europe, indeed in the world.

This special beer with the variety denomination "Kölsch" is a pale beer, similar in color to a pilsner, but unlike the latter it is made with top-fermenting yeast.

   As soft water is especially well-suited for brewing, this type of beer is very dependent on water. The name *"Kölsch"* may only be used for beers brewed in Cologne, which is why we print the name in quotation marks. Of course you can make this beer at home. The specific gravity of *Kölsch* beers is about 11°-12°. Lagering time is about 4-6 weeks. A variant of the above-cited *Kölsch* may and can be made with wheat malt. A maximum portion of 15% is used, which gives the beer a livelier note, a paler color and better head formation. Like the copper-colored *Altbier*, *Kölsch* is drunk from small (0.2 liter) glasses.

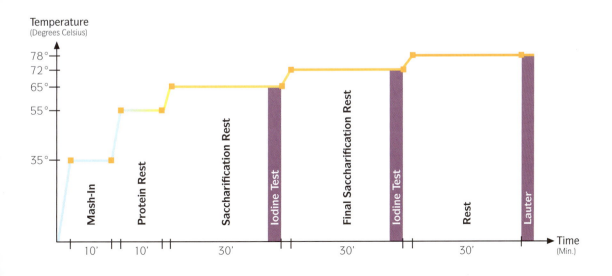

Export Beer
(bottom-fermented beer)

Ingredients for 10 liters of beer

2.5 kg	pale malt (Dortmunder)
100 g	caramel malt
14 g	hops (pellets)
7 liters	water
Sparge	8-10 liters of water
Dry or liquid yeast (bottom-fermenting)	

Ingredients for 20 liters of beer

5 kg	pale malt (Dortmunder)
200 g	caramel malt
25 g	hops (pellets)
13 liters	water
Sparge	12-14 liters of water
Dry or liquid yeast (bottom-fermenting)	

Mash-in at 35° C
Protein rest at 55° C (15 min.)
Raise temperature to 65° C
30 min, saccharification rest (iodine test!)
Raise temperature to 72° C
30 min. final saccharification rest (iodine test!)
Raise temperature to 78° C
30 min. rest, then lauter
Sparge with 78° C water to wash
the residual sugar from the mash

Boil with hops. Divide hops into three additions.
Filter and cool and then add the bottom-fermenting yeast.

Fermenting time about 8 days.
Lagering time at least 6 weeks.

With an output of more than six-million hectoliters (158,500,000 gallons) of beer annually, Dortmund is the undisputed beer capital, not just of Germany but of all of Europe. The term "Dortmunder" is a quasi designation of origin which covers all the beers produced by the approximately 30 breweries in Dortmund.

The pale, bottom-fermented beer classified under the term "Dortmunder Exportbier" has an specific gravity of about 13°. It differs from pilsners, which are also pale, in that it has a somewhat higher alcohol content but is less hopped.

Beers of this style are no longer only brewed in Dortmund; instead this somewhat stronger beer has earned a place alongside the other three big bottom-fermented beers, the pilsner, the Munich, and the Vienna Lager.

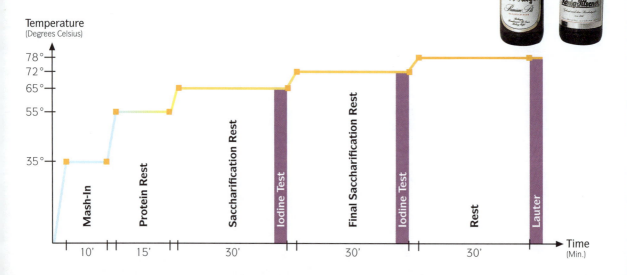

Temperature
(Degrees Celsius)

78° / 72° / 65° / 55° / 35°

Mash-In — Protein Rest — Saccharification Rest — Iodine Test — Final Saccharification Rest — Iodine Test — Rest — Lauter

10'   15'   30'   30'   30'

Time (Min.)

Roggenbier
(Rye Beer, top-fermented)

Ingredients for 10 liters of beer
1.5 kg	pale malt
700 g	rye (adjunct or malted)
30 g	hops (pellets)
8 liters	water
Sparge	8-10 liters of water
Dry or liquid yeast (top-fermenting)	

Mash-in at 40° C
Protein rest at 55° C (15 min.)
Raise temperature to 65° C
30 min, saccharification rest (iodine test!)
Raise temperature to 72° C
30 min. final saccharification rest (iodine test!)
Raise temperature to 78° C
30 min. rest, then lauter
Sparge with 78° C water to wash
the residual sugar from the mash

Ingredients for 20 liters of beer
3 kg	pale malt
1.5 kg	rye (adjunct or malted)
30 g	hops (pellets)
14 liters	water
Sparge	12-14 liters of water
Dry or liquid yeast (top-fermenting)	

Boil with hops. Divide hops into three additions.
Filter and cool and then add the bottom-fermenting yeast.

Fermenting time about 2-3 days.
Lagering time about 2 weeks.

The use of rye for making beer has at least as long a history as barley; however, its importance waned after the publishing of the German Purity Law. This grain is much used for home brewing, simply because rye, along with oats and spelt, is cultivated as a bread cereal in the rural areas of higher regions.

For brewing at home you can use rye as an adjunct, however the percentage of rye cannot exceed about 20% of the entire grain bill.

A higher percentage of adjunct is problematic, as the enzymes in the barley malt have to convert the starch in the crushed rye into sugar. The barley malt should therefore be as fresh as possible, in order to have the maximum amount of enzymes. A minimum of 50% barley malt is also necessary for filtering reasons. Rye malt is difficult to obtain, as only a few breweries brew this special beer and they obtain rye from the malters in their orders. When brewing with adjuncts, make sure that the grain, which is significantly heavier than the malt, does not settle on the bottom of the mash pot and burn, otherwise this will give the beer an unpleasant taste.

The taste of rye beer is most comparable to that of wheat beer, but it has a rather more robust and full flavored.

Of course, you can use other grains instead of rye, taking care not to exceed the specified percentage for adjuncts. The most important grains for the production of more eccentric beers are oats, spelt and emmer.

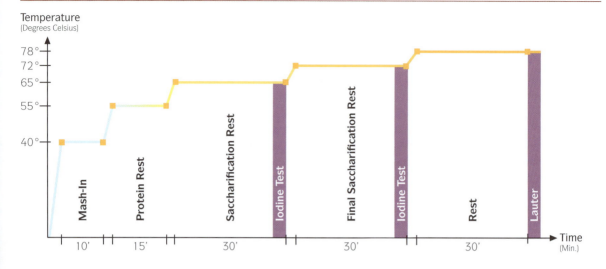

Temperature
(Degrees Celsius)

78°
72°
65°
55°
40°

Mash-In

Protein Rest

Saccharification Rest

Iodine Test

Final Saccharification Rest

Iodine Test

Rest

Lauter

10'   15'   30'   30'   30'

Time
(Min.)

"Rauchbier"
(Smoke Beer, top-fermented)

Ingredients for 10 liters of beer
2 kg   pale malt
300 g   roasted malt (over beech wood)
15 g   hops (pellets)
8 liters water
Sparge 8-10 liters of water
Dry or liquid yeast (top-fermenting)

Ingredients for 20 liters of beer
3 kg   pale malt
600 g   roasted malt (over beech wood)
30 g   hops (pellets)
14 liters water
Sparge 12-13 liters of water
Dry or liquid yeast (top-fermenting)

Mash-in at 40° C
Protein rest at 55° C (20 min.)
Raise temperature to 65° C
30 min, saccharification rest (iodine test!)
Raise temperature to 72° C
30 min. final saccharification rest (iodine test!)
Raise temperature to 78° C
30 min. rest, then lauter
Sparge with 78° C water to wash
the residual sugar from the mash

Boil with hops. Divide hops into three additions.
Filter and cool and then add the top-fermenting yeast.

Fermenting time about 2-3 days.
Lagering time about 3-4 weeks.

Nowadays *Rauchbiere* is a specialty of the Bamberg area. One must imagine that all beers must have tasted more or less of smoke before the invention of electric kilning, as the malt was kilned over an open fire and the malt must have taken on the taste of the smoke. This strong taste is not for everyone, for nowadays these flavor nuances are only common in smoked foods, especially sausage.

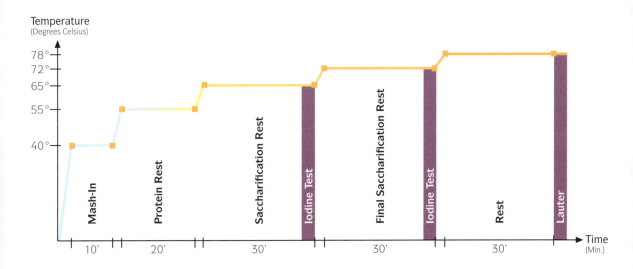

Austria

The history of beer in Austria is older than in many other countries of Europe, even though in parts of Austria wine is and was more popular. Beer and wine always coexisted harmoniously, however. They were never competitors, instead complementing each other marvelously.

Until well into the 19th century, less durable top-fermented beers were brewed in Austria—as elsewhere in the world. Then, in 1841, the Austrian Anton Dreher invented lager beer in Klein-Schwechat and the new style began its triumphal march around the world.

In the thousands of years from the days of the Sumerians to the present, nothing so permanently changed, indeed revolutionized, the making of beer as this "new beer" of Anton Dreher. Austria can therefore rightfully lay claim to being the birthplace of the modern brewing art, even though Czechoslovakian and, later, Bavarian brewers played a significant role in the subsequent development of this Vienna-style lager beer. Today, more than 80% of all the beer made in the world is brewed using this method developed in Austria, and brewers always refer to these beers as Vienna-style lager beers.

Austria soon became one of the biggest producers and exporters of beer in Europe, for until the end of the Danube monarchy such important brewing towns as Pilsen and Budweis lay within the territory of the Hapsburg Empire. This leading export role has not changed, indeed, since the fall of the Iron Curtain in 1989, this position has even improved as a result of takeovers of breweries or the issuing of licenses, thanks to the Austrian breweries' tradition of good contacts with Eastern Europe.

The Österreichischen Brau AG, a huge international brewing giant—now part of Heineken of the Netherlands—dominates the small Austrian domestic market. There are also many small, innovative regional breweries, and the recent years have seen a revival of *Gasthaus* breweries. With Austria's entry into the European Union in 1995, the market for beer—especially from neighboring Germany—opened. With a lower overall tax burden, the German breweries enjoyed significant competitive advantages over the Austrian breweries and their beers. There is certainly a need for action, for, especially in the regions bordering Bavaria in Upper Austria and Salzburg, direct imports of German beer have created sales problems for the Austrian breweries. The cause cannot be the quality of the Austrian beer, for the overwhelming majority of the small Austrian breweries consciously follow the strict terms of the German Purity Law.

In Austria, the making of beer is covered by the Codex alimentarius austriacus (Austrian Food Codex) and some of its regulations are significantly more restrictive than the corresponding rules in the German Beer Tax Law.

For example, in Austria any sort of chemical preparation of the brewing water, quite common in Germany, is forbidden. The excellent brewing water in Austria makes it possible to completely dispense with these chemical additives.

In addition to the classic lager beer, which, in Austria, is sold mainly under the name Märzenbier, many regional breweries make excellent pilsners, for they have access to the very soft water of the Bohemian Massif, the same water used in Pilsen and Budweis in the Czech Republic, especially in Upper Austria. Excellent brewing water, fresh water from the Alps, is available everywhere in Austria, and it can usually be used for brewing with no need for pre-treatment. Most Austrian beers are very pale, bottom-fermented beers, most of them brewed using hops grown in Austria. The most important hop-growing areas in Austria are in the Mühlviertel, the Waldviertel, and around Leutschach in southern Styria.

Märzen
(bottom-fermented beer)

Ingredients for 10 liters of beer

2.2 kg	pale malt (Vienna mixture)
15 g	hops (pellets)
8 liters	water
Sparge	8-10 liters of water
Dry or liquid yeast (bottom-fermenting)	

Ingredients for 20 liters of beer

4.3 kg	pale malt (Vienna mixture)
30 g	hops (pellets)
14 liters	water
Sparge	10-12 liters of water
Dry or liquid yeast (bottom-fermenting)	

Mash-in at 40° C
Protein rest at 55° C (15 min.)
Raise temperature to 65° C
30 min, saccharification rest (iodine test!)
Raise temperature to 72° C
30 min. final saccharification rest (iodine test!)
Raise temperature to 78° C
30 min. rest, then lauter
Sparge with 78° C water to wash
the residual sugar from the mash

Boil with hops. Divide hops into two or three additions.
Filter and cool and then add the bottom-fermenting yeast.

Fermenting time about 7-8 days.
Lagering time about 4-5 weeks.

This beer's specific gravity is about 12°.

Pale, bottom-fermented *Märzenbier* is brewed mainly in Austria and Bavaria and differs from pilsners, which are also made there, in that significantly less hops are used in its making.

Incidentally the name *"Märzenbier"* comes from the month of March (März), for until the 19th century, which saw the invention of electric refrigeration, this was the last month in which it was possible to brew longer-lasting bottom-fermented beers.

Not until the advent of electric refrigeration did it become possible to brew bottom-fermented beer all year long regardless of the weather.

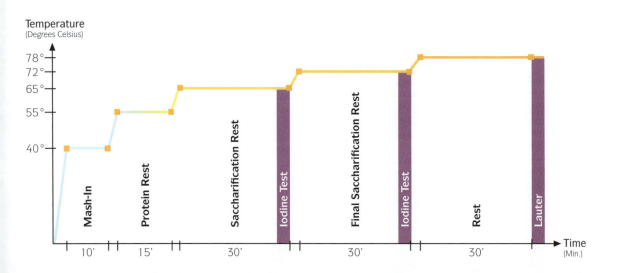

Dinkelbier
(Spelt Beer, top-fermented)

Ingredients for 10 liters of beer
1.5 kg   pale malt (Vienna mixture)
700 g   spelt (unmalted)
15 g   hops (pellets)
8 liters   water
Sparge   8-10 liters of water
Dry or liquid yeast (top-fermenting)

Ingredients for 20 liters of beer
4 kg   pale malt (Vienna mixture)
1.5 kg   spelt (unmalted)
30 g   hops (pellets)
14 liters   water
Sparge   10-14 liters of water
Dry or liquid yeast (top-fermenting)

Mash-in at 45° C
Protein rest at 55° C (15 min.)
Raise temperature to 65° C
30 min, saccharification rest (iodine test!)
Raise temperature to 72° C
30 min. final saccharification rest (iodine test!)
Raise temperature to 78° C
30 min. rest, then lauter
Sparge with 78° C water to wash
the residual sugar from the mash

Fermenting time about 2-3 days.
Lagering time about 3-4 weeks.

Spelt is one of the oldest varieties of grain cultivated by man and along with emmer was used by the Egyptians and Babylonians to make bread as well as beer. Like all grains, with the exception of malting barley, spelt was forced into the background by the terms of the German Purity Law. Not until recently did several breweries in Germany and Austria begin producing beer with the addition of spelt.

For use as an adjunct in home brewing, you can obtain spelt in health food stores and drugstores. Remember that like all adjuncts, unmalted spelt is significantly heavier than barley malt.

It therefore sinks to the bottom of the mash pot, where it can collect and burn, which produces an unpleasant taste.

In terms of taste, this spelt beer is most comparable to wheat beers, which are also produced with an adjunct and fermented with top-fermenting yeast.

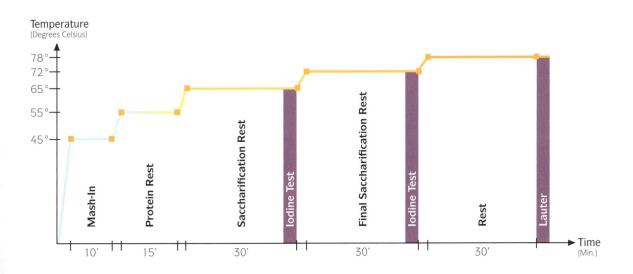

Hanfbier
(Hemp Beer, top-fermented)

Ingredients for 10 liters of beer

2.5 kg	pale malt
125 g	caramel malt
15 g	hemp (dried)
5 g	hops (pellets)
7 liters	water
Sparge	8-10 liters of water
Dry or liquid yeast (top-fermenting)	

Ingredients for 20 liters of beer

5 kg	pale malt
250 g	caramel malt
30 g	hemp (dried)
10 g	hops (pellets)
13 liters	water
Sparge	12-13 liters of water
Dry or liquid yeast (top-fermenting)	

Mash-in at 35° C
Protein rest at 55° C (15 min.)
Raise temperature to 65° C
30 min, saccharification rest (iodine test!)
Raise temperature to 72° C
30 min. final saccharification rest (iodine test!)
Raise temperature to 78° C
30 min. rest, then lauter
Sparge with 78° C water to wash
the residual sugar from the mash

Boil with hops and dried hemp leaves.
Divide hops into two or three additions.
Filter and cool and then add the top-fermenting yeast.

Fermenting time about 2-3 days.
Lagering time about 2-3 weeks.

This hemp-malt drink is made from an old brewing tradition, in which the hemp (*Cannabis sativa*) largely takes over the function of the hops and serves as a seasoning.

The unusual combination of hemp, hops, and malt gives the beer a slightly sweet, full-mouthed flavor. You also do not need to fear becoming "high" after enjoying this beer creation, for the contents of this old agricultural product, which is used to make clothing and whose growing is even promoted by the EU, are far below the allowable values contained in the applicable narcotic drug laws. On the contrary, its intoxicating effect is due to the alcohol content of the beer. Hemp leaves in pressed form, usually from organic farms, are available in many health food stores.

Switzerland

Most of the beers produced in Switzerland are lagers or the somewhat stronger special beers, precisely in the Alemanic-Bavarian tradition.

The Swiss brewing tradition is traceable back to the 9th century, from which time there are writings of the monastery brewery in St. Gallen. Founded by Irish missionaries during the Christianization of central Europe, the monastery in eastern Switzerland was one of Europe's first brewing centers, from which knowledge about brewing was spread through the founding of additional monasteries and missionary activity. A plan of St. Gallen from the year 814 shows three breweries on the premises of the monastery. The plan shows that the brewing areas had already been divided into different rooms. At that time more than 100 monks and numerous assistants worked in these three breweries, which all brewed a different beer.

Starkbier (strong beer) and Bockbier also have a tradition in Switzerland. The Hürliman Brewery in Zurich produces Samiclaus, the strongest beer in the world.

The alcohol content of this beer is an almost unbelievable 14% by volume. As its name suggests (Nicholas), this beer is only brewed on the 6th of December each year and then after fermentation it is lagered for one year and only consumed on the 6th of December the following year. A year appears on the label, as on wine bottles. Brewing this beer requires plenty of understanding and skill on the part of the brewer, for with such a high specific gravity there is the danger that the beer yeast will suffer from so-called yeast shock and become inactive. Unfortunately, such strong beers are not well suited for brewing at home, and we would therefore like to offer the recipe for a typical Swiss beer.

Special Beer
(bottom-fermented beer)

Ingredients for 10 liters of beer
2.5 kg   pale malt
125 g   caramel malt
13 g   hops (pellets)
7 liters   water
Sparge   8-10 liters of water
Dry or liquid yeast (bottom-fermenting)

Ingredients for 20 liters of beer
5 kg   pale malt
250 g   caramel malt
25 g   hops (pellets)
13 liters water
Sparge   12-13 liters of water
Dry or liquid yeast (bottom-fermenting)

Mash-in at 35° C
Protein rest at 55° C (15 min.)
Raise temperature to 65° C
30 min, saccharification rest (iodine test!)
Raise temperature to 72° C
30 min. final saccharification rest (iodine test!)
Raise temperature to 78° C
30 min. rest, then lauter
Sparge with 78° C water to wash
the residual sugar from the mash

Boil with hops. Divide hops into two additions.
Filter and cool and then add the yeast.

Fermenting time about 8-9 days.
Lagering time for this specialty beer is 5-6 weeks.

This beer's specific gravity is about 14°.
This full-mouthed, somewhat stronger and darker beer has a stronger taste than pale lager beers.

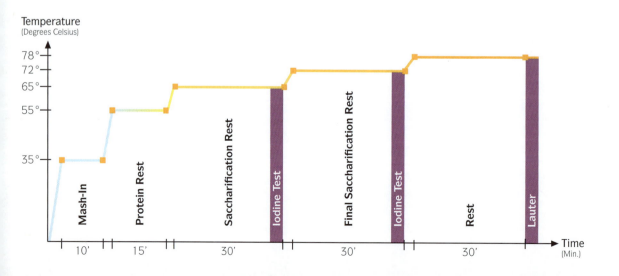

Czech Republic

The Czech Republic can also be considered one of the cradles of the modern brewing art. Its two famous beer towns, Budweis and Pilsen, were and are a guarantee of good beer. Pilsner, or more accurately Pilsner-style, beer is probably the most famous beer in the world and, of course, is no longer brewed just in Pilsen.

The wonderful soft brewing water of the Bohemian Massif and the hops from the world-famous Saaz agricultural region give these beers their unmistakable dry-bitter flavor nuances. The most-produced beer in the world, Budweiser by Anheuser-Busch of the USA, it owes its name to the Czech town of Budweis.

The Czech Republic is also by far the world leader in per capita beer consumption, even though the beers in the Czech Republic were traditionally brewed somewhat lighter than the 12° specific gravity usual in Central Europe. For example, *Pilsner Urtyp*, which is brewed by the brewery in Pilsen and protected by trademark law, has an specific gravity of just 11°. During the years of the communist state-controlled economy, the export of *Original Budweiser* and *Pilsner Urtyp* beers and Saaz hops was one of the most important sources of income of the former Czechoslovakia. Since the fall of communism, these two traditional beer-producing towns have struggled to regain the export success of their justifiably famous beers. Our selection for a representative Czech beer is of course a pilsner. Although excellent pilsners are now made around the world, because of its name this beer will always be linked with the Czech brewing town that gave it its name.

Brew shops offer malt mixtures described as pilsner mixture, and in order to come as close to the original pilsner as possible, we recommend that you use only Saaz hops, which are available for home brewing.

The brewing water in Pilsen has a hardness of only 20 mg CaO/l, which means that the softer the water you have at home, the closer you will come to the original. *Pilsner Urtyp* was first made in 1842, and after Anton Dreher's lager beer made in Kleinschwechat near Vienna, it was one of the first bottom-fermented beers in the world. *Original Pilsner* differs from the extremely bitter and very pale pilsner beers of northern Germany in that it is significantly darker and not as bitter because of the exclusive use of Saaz hops.

Pilsner Beer
(bottom-fermented)

Ingredients for 10 liters of beer
2.2 kg   pale malt (Pilsen mixture)
25 g   Saaz hops (pellets)
8 liters water
Sparge   6-7 liters of water
Dry or liquid yeast (bottom-fermenting)

Ingredients for 20 liters of beer
4.3 kg   pale malt (Pilsen mixture)
50 g   Saaz hops (pellets)
14 liters water
Sparge   8-10 liters of water
Dry or liquid yeast (bottom-fermenting)

Mash-in at 35° C
Protein rest at 55° C (10 min.)
Raise temperature to 65° C
30 min, saccharification rest (iodine test!)
Raise temperature to 72° C
30 min. final saccharification rest (iodine test!)
Raise temperature to 78° C
30 min. rest, then lauter
Sparge with 78° C water to wash the residual sugar from the mash

Boil with hops.
Divide hops into three additions.
Filter and cool and then add the bottom-fermenting yeast.

Fermenting time about 7-8 days.
Lagering time 5-6 weeks.

The specific gravity of this classic, bitter-dry beer is about 11°. The lagering period for the bottom-fermented beer is 5-6 weeks. Use the appropriate glasses for this special beer to enhance the head created by the Saaz hops.

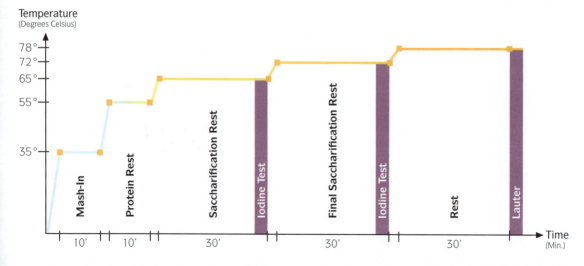

Great Britain

As a result of centuries of "splendid isolation", Great Britain developed its own beer traditions, which differed very clearly from the development of beer brewing on the Continent. Of course, there are also bottom-fermented beers in Great Britain, which are enjoying growing popularity, nevertheless nowhere else has the old beer culture remained so unadulterated as on the island. While these beers—served lukewarm, with no head, little carbon dioxide, and filled to the rim of the glass in pubs —do not exactly approach our taste in beer, these high-quality products are most probably comparable to the Belgian beers.

The classic beers of the British Isles, ales, stouts, and porters are top-fermented and are therefore easier to replicate at home than the bottom-fermented beers of Central Europe.

Brewing at home has a centuries-long tradition in Great Britain and many of these hobby brewers are organized into beer clubs and associations.

The problem for home brewing is that the malt mixtures used to make these typical English beers are unfortunately not—or not yet—available from mail order companies in Germany, Austria, and Switzerland. Liquid malt mixtures as semi-finished products or complete mixtures with hops are very probably obtainable. Unlike Central Europe, where unfertilized female umbels of the hops are used exclusively for beer making, in Great Britain male umbels are also used, giving the finished beer a somewhat different taste. If you have the opportunity during a visit to Great Britain, we recommend that you pick up some malt. Otherwise use a liquid malt mixture, which better reproduces the flavor nuances of English beers than the malts produced in our region. We have taken this into account in our recipe, which can be made with these mixtures, and have briefly explained how to make beer using liquid malt extract. Various malt mixtures, for example ale, bitter and stout, are usually available. Detailed instructions are often provided on the malt can, especially the amount of water required.

There are also slightly different mixtures for Irish (Guinness) and Scottish beers, which are made using whiskey malt and therefore have a slightly different flavor than English beers. The two most important drinks to the Scots are both made from barley—beer and whiskey.

Ale, Stout and Bitter
(top-fermented beer)
Liquid Malt Extract Mixtures

The liquid malt extract—a brown, sugary liquid—is dissolved by stirring in the indicated quantity of water. As the sugar has already been extracted from the malt (this process takes place in the malting factory), in this form of beer making the time-consuming process of mashing and lautering is eliminated. Hops are added to the dissolved malt and the wort is subsequently boiled for 1 to 2 hours. In order to initiate an optimal fermentation, the addition of a more or less large amount of sugar is necessary.

Several different malt mixtures, primarily ale, bitter, stout and porter, are available from specialty shops. Of course, there are other mixtures, such as pilsner and wheat beer, which can be made following the above-described procedure.

In addition to these semi-finished products there are also finished products that even contain the hops in dissolved form. In this case all that needs to be done is to add the specified amount of water and boil the wort. I leave it to the reader to decide to what extent these instant beers conform with the making of beer described in this book.

(Photo: www.holzeis.com)

Ireland

This book would be incomplete if its list of specialty beers failed to mention the Irish beer—Guinness. But Guinness is more than an extraordinary beer; instead it is an expression of the Irish philosophy of life, which they have exported worldwide with this beer. While Ireland is one of the small players in world beer production as far as per capita consumption is concerned, the Irish are nevertheless clearly in the leading group.

Guinness
(top-fermented beer)

The Guinness—the Irish beer—is produced from special toasted dark malt which gives it its characteristic coffee-like taste and its unique black color with the creamy-white head. As an original beer, it is made using the top-fermentation method, even though for export it is usually pasteurized or even brewed under license and consequently tastes somewhat different than in an Irish pub.

For brewing at home the same applies as for the making of English beers. Unfortunately the original malt is not available in brew shops or is very hard to obtain. Consequently it is recommended that you import it from England or Ireland or turn to one of the previously-mentioned liquid malt extract mixtures. If you have access to the internet you can locate several current suppliers of such liquid malt extract mixtures, just as recipes for these British and Irish beers can be found on the internet.

Scandinavia

As far as we Central Europeans are concerned, Scandinavia—and here we mean primarily Sweden, Norway and Finland—have no great beer-making tradition, as we are familiar with the Scandinavians' restrictive alcohol laws. Nevertheless beer is brewed in these three northern countries, divided into classes which in terms of specific gravity and percentage of alcohol by volume are closer to our light and alcohol-free beers.

Denmark is an exception. Following the Central-European tradition, the Danes brew bottom-fermented beers. Tuborg and Carlsberg dominate the market and these two big companies are also active internationally. Licensed production makes these beers available, not just in Germany, but also in the classic vacation countries of the Mediterranean and even in the U.S. The bottom-fermenting yeast (*Saccaromyces carlsbergensis*) takes its name from the Danish brewery of the same name.

Home brewing in the Scandinavian countries is also forbidden by law and is therefore restricted to the rural areas. As no hops grow in the Scandinavian climate, a mixture of juniper seeds or oak bark is still used as a bittering agent, similar to the additives used in Germany prior to the introduction of the Purity Law. Malting barley also has its climatic limits, consequently other types of grain, such as hardier rye and oats, are used for brewing.

Oat Beer
(top-fermented beer)

Ingredients for 10 liters of beer	
1.5 kg	pale malt
0.7 kg	oats (adjunct)
15 g	hops (pellets)
8 liters	water
Sparge	8-10 liters of water
Dry or liquid yeast (top-fermenting)	

Mash-in at 45° C
Protein rest at 55° C (15 min.)
Raise temperature to 65° C
30 min, saccharification rest (iodine test!)
Raise temperature to 72° C
30 min. final saccharification rest (iodine test!)
Raise temperature to 78° C
30 min. rest, then lauter
Sparge with 78° C water to wash
the residual sugar from the mash

Ingredients for 20 liters of beer	
3 kg	pale malt
1.4 kg	oats (adjunct)
30 g	hops (pellets)
14 liters	water
Sparge	10-12 liters of water
Dry or liquid yeast (top-fermenting)	

Boil with hops. Divide hops into two to three additions. Juniper seeds or dried oak bark can be used in place of hops. Use caution, as these bittering agents are significantly stronger than hops.
Filter and cool and then add the yeast.

Fermenting time about 2-3 days.
Lagering time for this specialty beer is 1-2 weeks.

The specific gravity of this beer is about 12°.

Russia

We in Central Europe do not think of Russia as a beer-producing country, our understanding of beer in the east ending in Budweis and Pilsen in the Czech Republic. But a beer tradition did develop in Russia—it is not a great deal different from that of Central Europe—though many beers are imported or brewed under license. Due to its climate, Russia has a much more marked culture (or perhaps one should say lack of culture) in the production if high-quality alcohols—schnapps and vodka, especially as one cannot forget the problems associated with the over-consumption of alcohol.

In this book about specialty beers we would like to introduce you to kvass (there are several other spellings, such as kwaas or kvaß—a drink that is similar to beer. While it lacks several of the elements that give beer its distinctive flavor, its basic composition has a very long tradition.

The Babylonians, Assyrians, and, later, the Egyptians did not use malt to make beer, instead using the processed form of the grain—bread. This old tradition lives on in *kvass*. Bread, usually black bread in Russia, is dried, crumbled, and placed in hot water. After filtering, sugar and yeast are added, and, after the first vigorous fermentation, the *kvass* is bottled and stored cool for several days.

Beer yeast is not necessarily used to make *kvass*. Normal bread yeast, which is closely related to beer yeast, is used instead.

The biggest difference between kvass and beer is that no hops are used to give the former a taste similar to that of beer. Instead raisins, fruit juices, lemon slices or honey are added to the wort.

Here your inventiveness and freedom to experiment are wide open, especially as this alcoholic beverage is not subject to the conditions of the German Purity Law, as it is not offered as a beer.

Kvaas
(top-fermented beverage similar to beer)

Ingredients for 10 liters of kvass
500 g   black bread
250 g   sugar
2 EL   raisins
12 liters boiling water
1 package of dry yeast or
one cube of yeast (baking yeast)

This beer-like beverage is made as follows:

Cut the black bread into slices and dry thoroughly in the oven. Old, dry bread can of course also be used. The dried bread is removed from the oven and crumbled by hand. Place 12 liters of boiling water in the mash pot and dissolved the crumbled dried bread in it. Let it soften in the water for 3-4 hours, until it has cooled. Then filter the liquid like beer, using a cloth diaper or tablecloth, squeezing the bread thoroughly. Afterwards add 250 g of sugar to the liquid, dissolve it by stirring vigorously and add yeast.

Very soon a vigorous fermentation will begin, similar to that described in the making of top-fermented beer, lasting about 7 to 8 hours depending on the sugar content. Afterwards bottle the kvass, adding three or four raisins to each bottle. They will rise in the bottle, showing that the kvass has already fermented out. As with beer, subsequent secondary fermentation in the bottle should produce sufficient carbon dioxide and of course alcohol to give the drink its refreshing sweet-sour taste. Without carbon dioxide and a head, kvass tastes flat and unattractive—like flat beer.

Kvass should spend 3-4 days in the refrigerator before it is drunk.

Brew Report

BREW NUMBER: _____   **DATE:** _____

TYPE: ☐ M   ☐ SP   ☐ P   ☐ B

M		kg	gal/hl	°F/°C	min.	Time	%
Malt	Grain						
	Boil						
Hops	1st Addition						
	2nd Addition						
	3rd Addition						
	Lactic Acid						
	Gypsum						
	Mash-In						
	pH						
	Heat to						
	Rest						
	Tun						
	Heat to						
	Rest						
	Heat to						
	Boil						
	Infusion						
	Lauter Rest						
	First Wort						
	1st Sparge						
	2nd Sparge						
	3rd Sparge						
	Last Wort						
	Boil start at						
	Boil						
	Strike out at (???)						
	pH						

NOTES:

BEER BREWER: _____

Legal Provisions

In the United States, home brewing is covered under the United States Code of Federal Regulations Title 27, Part 25, Subpart L, Section 25.205 and Section 25.206, as well as various statutes in the various states.

The U.S. Code:

Beer For Personal or Family Use

§ 25.205   Production.

(a) Any adult may produce beer, without payment of tax, for personal or family use and not for sale. An adult is any individual who is 18 years of age or older. If the locality in which the household is located requires a greater minimum age for the sale of beer to individuals, the adult shall be that age before commencing the production of beer. This exemption does not authorize the production of beer for use contrary to State or local law.

(b) The production of beer per household, without payment of tax, for personal or family use may not exceed:

(1) 200 gallons per calendar year if there are two or more adults residing in the household, or

(2) 100 gallons per calendar year if there is only one adult residing in the household.

(c) Partnerships except as provided in §25.207, corporations or associations may not produce beer, without payment of tax, for personal or family use.

§ 25.206   Removal of beer.

Beer made under §25.205 may be removed from the premises where made for personal or family use including use at organized affairs, exhibitions or competitions such as homemaker's contests, tastings or judging. Beer removed under this section may not be sold or offered for sale.

As of 2013, all 50 states permitted home brewing. The state laws differ from state to state and should be researched. The American Homebrewers association is a useful resource for all home brewers. Their website is www. homebrewsassociation.org and the specific site for government regulations is: http://www.homebrewersassociation.org/pages/government-affairs/statutes.

German-speaking Countries:

In the German-speaking countries, beer tax is calculated and levied as a withholding tax based on the beer's specific gravity and graduated according to each brewery's output.

In Switzerland and Austria beer can be brewed at home without the need for official approval. The consumption of home production is also tax-free. Transfer to a third party—whether for payment, to friends or free of charge—is, however, liable to tax. In Austria precise information as to the rate and modality of payment can be obtained from the responsible customs office and in Switzerland from the Swiss Directorate General of Customs, Beer Tax Department, in Bern.

The situation is somewhat different in the Federal Republic of Germany, where for brewing at home a report must be submitted to the responsible customs office. This must include the date, your address, the quantity and type of beer you intend to make. The payment of beer tax follows later; it is based both on the quantity and the specific gravity of the beer made. In most cases (approx. 25 liters of regular beer per month) you will fall under the tax limit and not have to pay any tax. This does not, however, relieve you of the obligation to submit a report or corresponding tax declaration.

Another curiosity is that until 1986 it was illegal in the Federal Republic of Germany to disseminate instructions for brewing at home. This book could not even have been sold then. Furthermore it was illegal to sell raw materials (hops, malt and yeast) for the purpose of brewing beer. You could buy all the necessary materials, together or separately, but the seller could not tell you that they were sufficient to produce X liters of beer. These laws are one of the reasons why brewing at home was almost completely forgotten.

Glossary of Brewing Terms

Abzugsbier: In Austria beers with an specific gravity of 9-10° are designated *Abzugsbiere*.

Adjuncts: In addition to malted barley, unmalted grains are also used in beer making, on the one hand as substitutes such as rice or corn, or unmalted wheat as in Belgian wheat beers. Adjuncts are not particularly suitable for home brewing, as the heavier unmalted grain tends to settle to the bottom of the mash pot with the resulting danger of burning.

Alpha-Amylase: An enzyme that causes the breakdown of brewing malt into maltose (malt sugar) during mashing.

Ale beers: "Ale" is understood to be a typical English beer which is brewed top-fermented. In English pubs it is usually served with no head, slightly cloudy and rather warm. The word "ale" is a collective term for these typical English beers, with several differences with respect to strength. There are various classes of ale in England, such as mild, bitter, pale ale, brown ale, and barley wine (strong beer). Belgian wheat beers and German *Altbier* share the same tradition. Ales are also made in Scotland and Ireland with a somewhat different tradition.

Alcohol content: The alcohol content of a beer is indirectly related to its specific gravity. Depending on the strength of the beer this varies from 0.5% alcohol by volume in so-called alcohol-free beers to 14% in strong beers like the Swiss Samiclaus.

Altbier: A top-fermented specialty beer, slightly dark to copper color. This beer is drunk from special *Altbier* glasses. In taste and tradition, hence the name *Altbier* (old beer), it is similar to English ale and Belgian top-fermented beers. The most important *Altbier* regions of Germany are Dusseldorf, Hanover and Munster.

Aroma hops: Aroma hops are a special and consequently expensive type of hop used mainly for the production of pilsner beers. Important growing regions for these types of hops are Hallertau and Tettnang in Bavaria and Saaz in the Czech Republic.

Berliner Weiße: A top-fermented specialty beer with a wheat component, which is fermentation with a mixture of yeast and lactic acid bacteria. Before drinking, *Berliner Weiße* is mixed (cut) with raspberry (red) juice or waldmeister (green).

Beta amylase: The second enzyme, along with alpha amylase, responsible for turning the starch in brewing malt into maltose (malt sugar) and dextrin.

Beer: Beer is a carbonated alcoholic beverage made from cereals (starchy grains), hops and water. It is mashed and boiled and fermented by means of yeast.

Beer hydrometer: A measuring device for determining the amount of dissolved solids in the wort. The ratio of dissolved solids to water is expressed as a percentage. A gravity of 12% or degrees means that there are 12 parts of dissolved solids against 88 parts of water. Most hydrometers used for home brewing are calibrated to a temperature of 20° C.

Bock beer (*Bockbier*): This strong beer has a higher specific gravity. Bock beer is very full-mouthed, finely-hopped, alcohol rich and amber-colored. These strong beers are brewed for special occasions such as Easter and Christmas. In Austria strong beers with an specific gravity higher than 14° are classified as "*Bockbiere*".

Bottom-fermented beer: Nowadays the majority of beers in the world (about 80%) are brewed bottom-fermented. Bottom-fermenting yeasts ferment at 15-20° C. The advantage of bottom-fermented beer is its longer shelf life. They can be transported long distances with no loss in quality. The most important varieties are pilsners, *Märzen*, special and lager beers.

Bottom-fermenting yeasts: Bottom-fermenting yeasts (*Saccaromyces carlsbergensis*) ferment at temperatures of 4-8° C. In contrast to top-fermenting yeasts, fermentation lasts about 7-8 days. Nowadays bottom-fermenting yeasts are cultured in special laboratories. Any breweries patent their yeasts, ensuring their exclusive use in their beers.

Brew house: The brew house is where the mash is made and the wort is subsequently boiled.

Brewing: The process of boiling the wort.

Brewing log: A device for keeping a record of each brewing process. The brewing logs helps with quantity control and facilitates the identification of brewing errors. It is also useful in calculating tax that may be due. For home brewing the brewing log is mainly useful for identifying brewing errors.

Brewing water: It should be as soft as possible without organic or mineral contaminants. The pH value should be between 4 and 5. The softer the water is, the better suited it is for brewing purposes. Soft brewing water results in higher yields. If the brewing water is not up to these high standards, breweries use chemical and physical processes to treat it before brewing. Water makes up 88% of finished beer.

Caramel: Caramel is used to color top-fermented beers, especially wheat beers. Caramel is the only additive permitted under the German Purity Law.

Caramel malt: A special type of malt that gives beer its full-bodied taste.

Colored malt: A special type of malt which is used to color the beer. It should not make up more than 2% of the grain bill in order to avoid affecting the flavor of the finished beer.

Decoction method: Is a more complex brewing method than the infusion method usually used in home brewing. Part of the mash is removed and boiled separately in another pot and is subsequently added to the mash again. This brewing method results in a higher yield per batch than the simple infusion method.

Degree of hardness: Brewing water's degree of hardness is determined by its content of various salts, minerals and trace elements, which are absorbed quite naturally from the earth. The characteristics of brewing water are partially responsible for the taste of the beer and also help determine its quality.

Dextrin: Is a simple sugar formed by the enzymes in the brewing malt. It is not completely fermentable and gives the beer mouth feel.

Enzyme: Biocatalysts in the malt which break down the fermentable substances (maltose and dextrin). The more active the enzymes in the malt are, the faster and more successful the saccharification.

Fermentation: Fermentation or alcoholic fermentation is understood to mean the process by which malt sugar is converted by yeast into carbon dioxide and alcohol.

Fermentation vessel: Open vessel in which the beer is fermented. A buildup of foam on the surface is a characteristic of this kind of fermentation. At home this type of fermentation is usually carried out in an open vessel.

Fermentation tank: Fermentation tanks are closed fermentation vessels, as opposed to open fermentation vessels. The excess carbon dioxide created during fermentation escapes through an airlock. Modern breweries use closed fermentation tanks almost exclusively as they provide better control during fermentation.

Filtering: In breweries, the finished beer is filtered to remove trub and yeast sediment. The result is clear (or polished) beer. Unfiltered beers are slightly cloudy, but these added elements result in a greater number of calories. In breweries kieselgur filters are used to filter out the suspended solids. Home-brewed beer, which is not filtered, is slightly cloudy but more aromatic.

Green malt: Green malt is the interim product in the malting process after germination and before kilning. It contains more enzymes than kilned malt, however it cannot be stored. You can make green malt in your oven at home.

Hops: The hop plant (*Humulus lupulus*) belongs to the same family as hemp and gives beer its characteristic bitter taste. In Central Europe, unfertilized female umbels are predominantly used in beer making,, whereas in England male umbels are also used. The bitter substances found in hops have an antibacterial effect and are important for the consistency of the head. For brewing hops are used in the form of dried natural hops, pressed hop pellets or hop extract in dried or liquid form. Hops are divided into two varieties, aroma hops for special bitter beers and bittering hops. The most important hop-growing regions in Central Europe are Hallertau, Tettnang, Saaz, the area surrounding Leutschach in southern Styria and the Mühlviertel in Upper Austria.

Infusion method: A simple brewing method in which the temperature of the mash is raised to 78° C while observing precisely determined rest periods. The infusion method is the easiest to use and most suitable method for brewing at home.

Iodine test: This test is used to determine if starch conversion has taken place. Technically speaking one measures the starch breakdown and in turn determines if malt sugar has been formed. If the iodine solution turns yellow, this means that conversion is complete. Standardized iodine solution or 1% potassium iodide solution (iodine-colored, not clear!) is used for the iodine test. Standard medicinal iodine solution for the treatment of wounds may also be used to carry out the iodine test. This iodine solution is inexpensive and may be purchased in any pharmacy.

Kilning: The drying or roasting process in the malthouse. The germinated grain is usually dried (kilned) with hot air. Pale malt is kilned at about 80° C, whereas dark malt is roasted at temperatures in excess of 105° C.

Kölsch: A specialty beer from Cologne which originally could only be brewed in this city on the Rhine. "*Kölsch*" is a top-fermented beer.

Kvass: A Russian beverage similar to beer, which is made by boiling black bread in water and adding baker's yeast. The process used to make this drink is similar to the original methods of making beer used by the Sumerians, Assyrians and Egyptians.

Lambic: Lambic beers are top-fermented Belgian specialty beers which are fighter without the use of cultured yeast. The wild yeast (spontaneous fermentation) give this unusual beer its special character. Sometimes Lambic beer is cut with fruit beer (cherry, strawberry or raspberry). Post-fermentation of these specialty beers takes place in the bottle in a manner similar to champagne, in the form of a second fermentation. Lambic beers are also placed in champagne bottles and sealed with corks.

Lautering: The separation of the solid components (grist) from the liquid components (wort) of the mash.

Light beer: This type of beer is relatively new and it has a less intense flavor than other types of beer. It is light (fewer calories and less alcohol) and is usually drunk colder than regular beers. Light beers have a maximum specific gravity of 9°.

Liquid malt: This form of malt spares the home brewer the time-consuming task of mashing. Liquid malt is sold in cans or glass jars. These "pre-brewed" malts are ideal for your first brewing attempts.

Malt: Created by special processing of malting barley in malthouses. The malting barley is soaked in water, which causes it to germinate. The water is constantly aerated, which prevents the malt from going moldy. After several days the malting process is ended and the malt is kilned (dried)—pale malt at about 70° C and dark malt at more than 100° C (roasted).

Malthouse: The malthouse used to be an important part of every brewery. Nowadays the profession of malter is separate from that of brewer, and malthouses operate as service companies on behalf of the breweries. In malthouses two-row summer barley is sprouted and subsequently roasted to produce various kinds of malt. Pale brewing malt is kilned (dried) at about 70° C, while dark malt is roasted at over 100° C.

Malting barley: For the most part two-row summer barley is used for brewing beer. It is readied for the brewing process in the malt house. More than 300 different varieties of malting barley are grown worldwide. Malting barley differs from feed barley in that it has significantly more starch and less protein.

Maltose (malt sugar): In the mashing process, enzymes in the malt convert starch into maltose (malt sugar). The yeast then turns the maltose into alcohol and carbon dioxide during fermentation. The concentration of maltose in the wort determines the strength of the beer.

Märzenbier: An unusually malty, mildly hopped, top-fermented beer typical for Austria and Bavaria. Incidentally the name *Märzenbier* (literally "March beer") comes from the month of March. Before the advent of artificial refrigeration, March was the last month of the year in which longer-lasting top-fermented beers could be made.

Mashing: The mixing of crushed brewing malt with water in the mash tun.

Mash tun: In a brewery a vat used for mashing. For home brewing the mash tun is usually a large cooking pot.

Micro brewery: Small breweries, usually with an attached restaurant, which have enjoyed rising popularity in recent years. These breweries usually serve unfiltered beer (*Zwicklbier*).

Nährbier: A substantially sweeter, maltier type of beer which is brewed using a special method, however it contains less alcohol than other regular beers with the same specific gravity.

Specific gravity: Expressed as a percentage or degrees, it indicates the amount of dissolved solids from the malt and hops present in beer. An specific gravity of 12°, for example, means that there are 12 parts dissolved solids against 88 parts water. The specific gravity, or specific gravity, is measured precisely using a beer hydrometer and is also the basis for calculating the beer tax. The specific gravity is not to be confused with the beer's alcohol content, although the latter is indirectly dependent on the former. As a rule of thumb, the specific gravity divided by three results in the approximate alcohol content of the beer.

pH value: An expression of the acid value of the brewing water. The optimal pH range for beer making is 4-5. To test the brewing water use pH test strips, which change color to indicate the water's acid value.

Pilsner beer: A bottom-fermented, very pale but strongly-hopped beer with an specific gravity of 11-13°. This variety takes its name from the Czech town of Pilsen, known for its excellent soft brewing water.

Polished beer: Clear, filtered beers, in contrast to unfiltered yeast beers. Most beers today are filtered before bottling. Polished beers contain fewer calories than unfiltered beers.

Porter: Porter, or Stout, is a dark top-fermented beer made with roasted malt. This beer originated in London and became popular, especially in Ireland, as "dry stout." Made in Dublin, Guinness is famous the world over.

Primary fermentation: Primary fermentation takes place in a fermentation vessel or tank. With a top-fermenting yeast primary fermentation lasts two to three days, while with a bottom-fermenting yeast primary fermentation lasts seven to eight days.

Purity Law: The "Purity Law" was issued by Duke Wilhelm IV of Bavaria on 23 April 1516. It prescribes the exclusive use of water, barley malt and hops in the making of beer. In 1516 no one knew that yeast was the fourth raw material in brewing. The only exception allowed by the Purity Law is the use of wheat malt in making *Weißbier*. Since 1918 the German Purity Law has applied to the entire Federal Republic and has also been adopted by many foreign breweries for making their beer.

Residual grain: The solid elements of the mash which are separated from the wort during lautering. A byproduct of the mashing process, it is used as a high-grade fodder as it contains large amounts of protein. At home the residual grain can be used to make muesli or as an additive in bread making. Some breweries also use this residual grain to distill a type of schnapps which tastes similar to Italian *Grappa* (which made from the pomace left over from wine making).

Rough-grind: The crushing of the malt kernels prior to the actual brewing process. The malt kernels are roughly ground, more specifically crushed rather than finely ground.

Saccharification rest: A pause in the mashing process, during which the enzymes in the brewing malt break down the starch into maltose (malt sugar) and dextrin.

Samichlaus beer: The strongest beer in the world, it is a Swiss specialty beer which is named after St. Nicholas because it is only brewed on the 6th of December and is not sold until a year later on that date. The year is stamped on the bottle label. This strong beer has an alcohol content of about 14% by volume.

***Schankbier*:** Beers with an specific gravity of 10-12° are designated *Schankbiere* (draught beers) by the Austrian Beer Tax Law.

Secondary fermentation: In breweries, secondary fermentation usually takes place in lagering tanks. Specialty beers, such as wheat beers, also undergo secondary fermentation in the bottle. With home-brewed beer, secondary fermentation always takes place in the bottle as home brewers do not have closed fermentation tanks, without which the carbon dioxide formed during secondary fermentation would escape during bottling.

Separation of cold break: After the wort is cooled, suspended solids consisting of protein components and hop remnants again precipitate from the wort and are filtered out prior to fermentation.

Separation of hot break: When the wort is boiled with the hops, protein remnants drop out of the wort. These are removed from the hot wort by means of a filter or whirlpool. When brewing at home these protein components can be filtered out using a cloth filter.

Simple beer (*Einfachbier*): In Germany beers with an specific gravity of 2 to 5.5° are designated simple beers.

Sparge water: Hot water which is added to the mash to dissolve important elements still in the grain. The sparge is mixed with the separated wort and together are boiled with the hops.

Speise: Part of the wort, which is added to the young beer after primary fermentation to promote secondary fermentation in the bottle, keg or can.

Stout: A very dark, almost black, beer, which is made with dark roasted malt. It has a taste comparable to coffee beans, as the malt is roasted in a similar process. The best-known representative of this top-fermented beer is the Irish Guinness beer, which is available almost worldwide, although the original brewed in Dublin tastes different than the beers brewed under license in other countries.

Strong beer (*Starkbier*): In Germany and Switzerland beers with an specific gravity greater than 14° are designated strong beers. In Austria, however, such beers are called "bock beers".

Sugar: In many beers that are not brewed according to the German Purity Law, a certain amount of sugar is added to the mash, replacing relatively expensive malt. Many home-brewing recipes from the Anglo-Saxon world call for the use of this additive. The well-known Trappist beers of Belgium and the Netherlands are post-fermented in the bottle with the addition of candy sugar.

Top-fermented beer: A beer brewed with fermenting yeast which ferments at 15-20° C. Top-fermented has the disadvantage of shorter shelf life and storability. Top-fermented beers were the most common type until the invention of electric refrigeration in the 19th Century. Nowadays mainly specialty beers are made using this method. The most important beer varieties of this kind are wheat beers, *Alt*, *Kölsch*, ale, porter and stout.

Top-fermenting yeasts: Top-fermenting yeasts (*Saccaromyces cerevisiae*) are the original brewing yeasts. They work at 15-20° C and when primary fermentation ends they settle on the surface of the fermentation vessel, hence their name. With these yeasts fermentation takes 2-3 days. As no expensive cooling is required, these yeasts are particularly well suited for home brewing.

Vollbier: In Germany beers with an specific gravity of between 11 and 14° are designated *Vollbiere*. This categorization also applies in Austria, with the name of the specific beer type—*Weißbier*, *Pils* or *Märzen*—taking precedence.

Weizenbier (wheat beer): A top-fermented beer with a wheat malt component of at least 50%. Wheat beer is sparkling and refreshing, weakly hopped and highly carbonated. There are both clear (*Weizenbock* and light) and yeast-clouded varieties. Bavarian *Weizenbier*—called *Weißbier* elsewhere in Germany—has enjoyed an unprecedented surge in popularity in recent years, especially during the warmer seasons. Wheat beers are also made in Belgium, though mostly with wheat as an adjunct (unmalted).

Wort: The liquid part of the mash which is boiled with the addition of hops.

Yeasts: Bio-organisms which cause fermentation by turning malt sugar into alcohol and carbon dioxide. There are two types of yeast used for brewing with different fermentation characteristics. Top-fermenting yeasts (*Saccaromyces cerevisiae*) ferment at 15-20° C and are the original beer yeasts. Today these are used mainly for specialty beers. Most modern-day beers are made with bottom-fermenting yeasts (*Saccaromyces carlsbergensis*), which require artificial (electric) cooling equipment as they work at temperatures of 4-8° C. Yeasts are so small that they can only be seen under a microscope at 800-fold magnification. For this reason, for a long time man was unaware that yeast was required for the making of beer. There is no mention of yeast in the German Purity Law of 1516.

Zwicklbier: Unfiltered beer that is removed from the fermentation vessel through a single tap, the so-called "Zwickl tap". Recently these unfiltered beers have been offered as a specialty and have enjoyed growing popularity, especially in micro-breweries. As these beers contain living yeast cells, they have a fuller and more intense flavor. They also have a higher caloric content, however.

Acknowledgments

I would first like to thank the readers of my first book, *Beer Brewing for Everyone*, who made it possible for this expanded version to be published. I would also like to thank the many people who took part in my beer brewing seminars in Austria and the Federal Republic of Germany. Their comments and suggestions helped me eliminate the weak points in the first book and add to it, especially from a technical point of view. I never cease to be surprised by the inventiveness of home brewers, who come up with ideas to make home brewing easier and more professional. No cost, effort or time was spared to improve the conditions for brewing—whether it is designing lauter tun or construction of a wort chiller from copper tubing.

I am especially grateful to Ing. Michael Holzeis (Kellereibedarf Knopf) for the pictures of raw materials and equipment for home brewing as well as for our interesting discussions about home brewing and the latest innovations. I also wish to thank my son Philipp Hlatky for his help with my "exhibition brewing" and photographing the brewing process.

Special thanks goes to the Leopold Stocker Verlag for the confidence they showed in me and for making it possible to so richly illustrate this book.

Literature

Delos, Gilbert: Biere aus aller Welt. Karl Müller Verlag, Erlangen 1994.

Friedrich, Ernst: Bier. Sigloch Edition, Künzelsau, 1993.

Hlatky, Christine: Kochen mit Bier. Leopold Stocker Verlag, Graz, Stuttgart, 2. Auflage 1996.

Hlatky, Michael: Das große österreichische Bierlexikon. Austria Medien Service, 2. Aufl., Graz, 1999.

Hlatky, Michael und Christine: Bierbrauen zu Hause. Mit Spezialitäten aus ganz Europa.

Leopold Stocker Verlag, Graz, Stuttgart, 1997.

Hlatky, Michael; Reil, Franz: Bierbrauen für jedermann. Leopold Stocker Verlag, Graz, Stuttgart, 5. Auflage 1997.

Hlatky, Michael; Walzl, Manfred: Jungbrunnen Bier, gesunder Genuss, Verlagshaus der Ärzte, 3. Auflage 2004.

Höllhuber, Dietrich; Kaul, Wolfgang: Die Biere Deutschlands. Verlag Hans Carl, München, 2. Auflage 1993.

Hübner, Regina und Manfred: Der deutsche Durst, illustrierte Kultur- und Sozialgeschichte. Edition Leipzig, Leipzig 1994.

Jackson, Michael: Bier International. Hallwag Verlag, Bern und Stuttgart 1994.

Jackson, Michael: Bier, über 1000 Marken aus aller Welt. Hallwag Verlag, Bern Stuttgart, 4. Aufl. 1994.

Lohberg, Rolf: Das große Lexikon vom Bier. Scripta Verlag, Stuttgart, 3. Auflage 1984.

Merk, Gerhard; Hannes, Sieber: Das Münchner Bier, Wer's braut, wie's schmeckt, wo's fließt. Frisinga Verlag, 1991.

Messing, Norbert: Heilen mit Bierhefe. Die Wiederentdeckung einer alten Volksarznei, Verlag Ganzheitliche Gesundheit, Bad Schönborn, 5. Aufl. 1993.

Narziß, Ludwig: Abriß der Bierbrauerei. Ferdinand Enke Verlag, Stuttgart, 4. Auflage 1980.

Rätsch, Christian: Urbock Bier jenseits von Hopfen und Malz. Von den Zaubertränken der Götter zu den psychedelischen Bieren der Zukunft. AT- Verlag, Aarau 1996.

Schramm, Manfred: Heilen mit Hopfen. Gesundheit aus einer alten Kulturpflanze. Ehrenwirth Verlag, München 1997.

Soyez, Konrad: Biotechnologie. Birkhäuser Verlag, Basel, Boston, Berlin 1990.

Vogel, Wolfgang: Bier aus eigenem Keller. Verlag Eugen Ulmer, Stuttgart, 3. Auflage 1993.

Wagner, Christoph: Bier & Küche. Guide-Verlags-Anstalt, 1987.

Photo Credits

Andrea Malek, Malanda-Buchdesign: 116
The Brewers of Europe, www.brewersof-europe.org: 28, 34, 38, 41, 60, 143
Chris Lang: 14, 27
DI Franz Reil: 22, 23
Dieter Gansterer: 93
Foto Tropper: 134
Hagen Schaub: 12, 152
Heike Pekarz: 30
Herwig Steiner: 42, 64
Hr. Klement: 127
Ing. Leopold Schlögl: 57, 103
Ing. Michel Holzeis: 32, 37, 48, 49, 56, 69, 70, 71, 72, 73, 74, 76, 77, 81,
      97, 100, 102, 108, 109, 126, 127, 128, 129, 163
Michael Hlatky: alle Ablauffotos
Osttiroler Getreidemühlen: 44
Philipp Hlatky: 183
Verband der Brauereien Österreichs: 21, 35

About the Author

After training as a master dry cleaner, Michael Hlatky studied business administration in Graz with emphasis on marketing. He has been active in the publishing field since 1985—as a marketing and sales manager, publisher, and, since 2003, as an independent publishing agent.

He has written and published several books on the topic of beer, including: *Beer Brewing for Everyone, Beer Brewing at Home, Beer Yeast for Health and Beauty, The Big Austrian Beer Lexicon*. He has also lectured on making beer and held brewing seminars.

Conversion Tables

With few exceptions such as ABV, exactness of measurement is not a requirement for making mead. This chart offers metric measures, with English equivalencies in more common terms as well as more accurate approximations. Conversion programs abound on the internet.

WEIGHT

Metric	U.S. Units ACCURATE	U.S./U.K. Common (EST.)
1 mg	.015 grains	–
2 mg	.031 grains	–
5 mg	.077 grains	–
10 mg	.154 grains	–
20 mg	.308 grains	–
30 mg	.462 grains	–
40 mg	.617 grains	–
50 mg	.771 grains	–
60 mg	.926 grains	–
70 mg	1.08 grains	–
80 mg	1.23 grains	–
90 mg	1.39 grains	–
100 mg	1.54 grains	–
1 g	0.04 oz	–
2 g	0.07 oz	–
3 g	0.10 oz	–
4 g	0.14 oz	–
5 g	0.18 oz	–
6 g	0.21 oz	–
7 g	0.25 oz	–
8 g	0.28 oz	–
9 g	0.32 oz	–
10 g	0.35 oz	–
20 g	0.70 oz	–
30 g	1.05 oz	–
40 g	1.40 oz	–
50 g	1.75 oz	–
100 g	3.5 oz	–
200 g	7.0 oz	–
500 g	17.5 oz	–
750 g	26.25 oz	–
1 kg	35 oz/2.2 lb	–
2 kg	4.4 lb	–
3 kg	6.6 lb	–
4 kg	8.8 lb	–
5 kg	11.0 lb	–
10 kg	22.0 lb	–
50 kg	110.3 lb	–
75 kg	165.3 lb	–
100 kg	220.5 lb	–

VOLUME

Metric	U.S. Units ACCURATE	U.S./U.K. Common (EST.)
50 ml	1.7 oz	10 teaspoons
100 ml	3.4 oz	7 tablespoons
125 ml	4.2 oz	7 tablespoons
250 ml	8.5 oz	0.5 cup
500 ml	17 oz	1 pint
1 liter	33.8 oz	1 quart
2 liters	67.7 oz	2 quarts
3 liters	101.4 oz	3 quarts
4 liters	135.5 oz	4 quarts/1 gallon
5 liters	169.1 oz	5 quarts
6 liters	202.9 oz	6 quarts
7 liters	236.7 oz	7 quarts
8 liters	270.5 oz	8 quarts/2 gallons
9 liters	304.3 oz	9 quarts
10 liters	338.1 oz	10 quarts
15 liters	507.2 oz	15 quarts
20 liters	676.3 oz	20 quarts/5 gallons
30 liters	1014 oz	30 quarts
40 liters	1353 oz	40 quarts/10 gallons
50 liters	1691 oz	50 quarts
50 liters	1691 oz	50 quarts
75 liters	2536 oz	75 quarts
100 liters	3381 oz	100 quarts
150 liters	5072 oz	150 quarts
200 liters	6763 oz	200 quarts/50 gallons